CHRIST CHURCH
COLLEGE
CANTERBURY

Into New Worlds

Sheila McCullagh

A guide to teaching reading

HART-DAVIS EDUCATIONAL

Granada Publishing Limited

First published in 1974
Hart-Davis Educational
Frogmore St Albans Hertfordshire AL2 2NF
and
3 Upper James Street London W1R 4BP

Copyright © 1974 Sheila McCullagh

ISBN 0 247 1254 90

Printed in Great Britain by
Northumberland Press Limited, Gateshead

Contents

PART THREE: LATE STARTERS

PART FOUR: DEVELOPING READING SKILLS

APPENDIX

Illustrations

Illustrations

Foreword

This book is intended as a guide for anyone who is faced with teaching the early stages of reading to children, perhaps for the first time, and who would be glad of some help in planning the experiences the children will need and the work to be done. There are a number of practical suggestions throughout the book which can be considered, tried out, adopted, adapted or discarded, according to the particular teacher's needs and those of the children concerned, but which in any case serve to illustrate the ideas being put forward. They do not attempt to cover everything a teacher might do; they simply serve to show how a principle may be worked out in practice, to give a beginner a starting point.

The importance of the teacher as a factor in learning to read is becoming more and more recognized. An article by Paul Widlake in *Remedial Education*, based on a survey of reading in some inner city schools, ended with the words: *no other single factor has the weight and significance of teacher performance.* (Widlake's italics.) Dr Vera Southgate has stressed the importance of what she calls a 'reading drive', which she describes as 'basically a new range of inspiration through the teaching of the subject'. If teachers in a school are actively concerned in helping children to learn to read, then the standards of reading in that school are likely to be good, no matter what method they follow. This does not mean that one method is as good as another: it does mean that the teacher is a vital part of the whole situation.

Into New Worlds is intended primarily for teachers, but it may also be of use to parents who like to understand what is happening in school, and perhaps be able to help their children if they can. It is an attempt to answer the question which is sometimes put to me: 'I have to teach reading: what should I do?' There is no golden rule to be followed without deviation, but one can plan a campaign, evaluating and continually revising and developing the plan as time goes on. The first plan is perhaps the most difficult one to work out, and this book is an attempt to help in its formulation.

Since the purpose of the book is to help teachers who may not yet have had an opportunity to teach children who are learning to read, notes on one or two books which experienced teachers have found to be specially helpful are included at the end of each chapter. These books sometimes present differing points of view, and this is all to the good. All of them contain a discussion of principles, practical suggestions and useful bibliographies for further reading. I have deliberately avoided many specific references to modern research into the teaching of reading in *Into New Worlds* for two reasons: because experience is necessary in evaluating research findings and in seeing their relevance to practice in the classroom, and because a long bibliography and list of references can discourage rather than encourage further reading, especially for the inexperienced teacher whose time and energy are already absorbed in teaching the children. But of course a background knowledge of the findings of relevant modern research is important, and some books are included with that in mind.

Schools and teachers vary in their approach to the teaching of reading. Some schools use a reading scheme which demands a special way of teaching (eg Gattengo's *Words in Colour*) and provides detailed instructions for the presentation of materials; but most use a flexible approach, a combination of methods, differing chiefly in emphasis, varied according to the needs of individual children and teachers—for it is important that both should have confidence in what they are doing. The suggestions outlined in this book can readily be adapted to fit in with the work in most primary schools, their special contribution being the emphasis placed on the importance of encouraging a thoughtful imaginative response from the children and on providing, from the very first books they encounter, stories and other reading material which really interests them within the context of a planned systematic approach.

PART ONE

Background to Reading

I

Establishing a Climate of Literacy

a UNDERSTANDING ROOTED IN EXPERIENCE

When a child learns to understand words, to speak and use a language, he takes a giant step forward in development. When he learns to read he takes another giant stride. If he learns well, he learns a skill which opens the door into new worlds of imagination and experience, worlds which he can enter when he chooses and explore according to his needs. Of all the skills we teach our children, the ability to handle spoken and written language is surely the most important, for through it they come into contact with the thoughts and feelings of other human beings. Reading is a skill which sets children free to think and find out for themselves, which gives them independence and at the same time increases their understanding of themselves and others and of the world in which they live.

A few children, surrounded by books and given help and encouragement, learn to read at home, but the vast majority learn at school. For most children there must be specific teaching, and this teaching is one of the most important responsibilities that falls on teachers, and not on teachers in infant schools alone: all the way through to the university and beyond, we learn, or should learn, more about how to read. But the responsibility for the beginnings of reading falls most heavily on teachers in infant and junior schools, because not only are most children learning the fundamentals of the skill during that period, but because they are also developing an attitude towards reading and what reading has to offer them. Attitudes which we develop when we are young can last a long time and are difficult to change once they are established, so that as teachers we do well to take a long view.

Although in these days other media, particularly TV and radio, provide children and adults with information and experience, they are still no substitute for books. Books are available whenever the individual needs them; they make independent investigation possible, for reading allows time for checking and considering ideas. Nowadays, when the publicity men are so skilled at creating an image, at 'selling a president', it is perhaps even more important to our way of life that citizens should be able to read critically and use their own imagination. There is a growing number of forms any effective citizen must be able to comprehend; a politician's speech on TV, with all the background arranged to sell an image, is more difficult to assess critically than the same speech read quietly; and a story or play, dressed by the producer's imagination, is not the same experience as the story read in a book, where the reader sets his own stage and peoples it with characters formed from all those he has himself encountered in life, where the author's commentary and the reader's reflections on his own experience can illumine the theme as it develops.

To be able to read thoughtfully and with imagination, critically appraising the text, distilling information, or interpreting it in terms of one's own experience in life, is just as important as it ever was and perhaps even more so. Impressions made in early childhood go deep. Few people in constructing courses in literature, or considering the place of reading in later life, look back to see what attitudes and ways of approach to books were developed by the teachers concerned with the children in their earliest years at school. They should.

In teaching even the very beginnings of the skill to children, there are two fundamental aspects of reading which it is wise to hold in mind. The first concerns the nature of reading. If a child (or indeed anyone) is to value reading, it must have significance for him:* it must convey interesting ideas and information, or widen and deepen his experience through his imagination, or at least provide him with recreation and amusement. It may well do all three. But the second aspect of reading has to be remembered by the teacher too: reading is a skill, or perhaps it would be truer to say a bundle of related skills. All we know about the learning of skills indicates that systematic presentation and sequential practice are important. You learn to swim only in the water, but you can practise strokes on dry land (and in the water too, with special supports to help you), provided you try out the strokes you have practised in the proper element later on. If you are simply

---

* Throughout the book, to avoid the clumsy 'he or she' and 'him or her', the teacher is referred to as 'she' and the child as 'he'.

thrown in at the deep end, you may drown or you may develop a fear of water; if you spend all your time playing about in the shallow end you may never learn to swim at all, let alone swim efficiently. Yet in teaching reading as a skill, we should always remember that it has significance only in use: just as you can only swim in water, so you can only read, in the full sense of the term, when you are surrounded by words which have meaning for you and from which you gain understanding.

Methods of teaching reading fall into two main groups: visual methods (sometimes called 'look and say', though this is something of a misnomer, since it refers only to one method of learning to recognize words, and visual methods make use of many and various techniques) and phonic methods. The great advantage of visual methods is that they can (though this does not always follow) use significant, meaningful material from the very beginning; the advantage of phonic methods is that (if taught effectively) they provide the children with a useful technique for reading a new word and encourage independence. To these a third should be added: kinaesthetic methods. Children also learn to recognize words by getting the feel of them, by writing and tracing them. Writing words draws the children's attention to their details, too, to their letters and combinations of letters, and so helps them to recognize and remember them. Reading and writing go together.

Any one of these methods may be dominant in the teaching of reading, though in practice most teachers use all three. Children vary in their abilities and some find it easier to learn in one way rather than another. Some teachers find that, for them, one method is more effective than another, because they use it more happily themselves. The important thing is never to lose sight of the aim of teaching: that reading should have a significant and valued part to play in living, that is, in the life of the children and adults, at whatever age they may be.

There are two good reasons why it is not possible to lay down hard and fast rules about the age at which a child should begin to learn to read: the first is that children and circumstances differ so much, that the age at which the teaching of reading can usefully start is bound to vary considerably between different groups of children and between individuals in the same group; the second is that reading does not begin suddenly, even though there may be marked stages in the process of learning. When a child first listens to and uses speech, he is laying the essential foundations for learning to read, for reading is part of the development of literacy, which includes spoken and written language. In teaching reading in school, we are building on a great deal of past experience, and where the necessary experience for a new stage is lacking, it is up to us as teachers to provide it if we can.

A Climate of Literacy

One of the first responsibilities a teacher has towards children who are learning to read is to establish a climate of literacy. By this I mean an environment in which reading is seen to be important by the children, because of the immediate satisfaction it brings them. We want children to value reading for something other than the adult approval it brings. Many children are aware of the value which adults put on children being able to read. Even people who do not read very much themselves seem frequently to judge a school's efficiency and a child's progress by his ability in reading. In places where there has been an immense change in the methods and content of learning since the parents went to school, the adults frequently grasp at reading ability as the one measure of progress which seems familiar and which they feel, rightly or wrongly, they can evaluate. (To be fair, even if they are sometimes mistaken they are surely right in this: reading is of fundamental importance to education and to living.) Adult approval means a very great deal to children, and it is not only parents and neighbours who approve ability in reading: the teacher's approval too is attracted by a child's success.

This adult approval is a great incentive to a child to learn to read, but it can create problems. If a child is unsuccessful, the lack of it can be so discouraging that a barrier is built up towards learning. Even for a child who learns easily, adult approval is a passing thing: the only lasting reason for learning to read is that reading is rewarding in itself. By setting out to make reading as immediately interesting and satisfying as we can, we are not setting out to create a soft option; we are trying to generate the energy necessary to carry the children through a long period of hard work. Human beings work best when they see that the results of their work are worthwhile, and we are prepared to undertake work which may not always be interesting in itself if we can see its value. Children are not different in this respect, though we cannot expect them to look a long way ahead; the greater their motivation, the harder we can expect them to work. But their goals, especially to begin with, have to be short term. They need to reach them quickly. The teacher will see or plan ahead, her long-term aim being to help the children to learn to read effectively; but the child's purpose may be at most to make a little book of his own, or to complete a pre-reader, perhaps only to print the caption below his picture. All of these things will demand effort and concentration from him.

Establishing a Climate of Literacy in the Informal School

There is no rigid line of demarcation between informal and formal schools: although the extremes at either end of the continuum are very different, in most primary schools there are times when the organization for learning is informal, and times when it is more systematic and carefully planned. But I have used the terms in this book to mean on the one hand schools where the work is developed from spontaneous interests of the children in a setting which allows them a great deal of freedom of movement and choice of occupation, and on the other hand, in the more formal setting, schools where the work and activities are planned by the teacher, though she will enlist the children's interest in what is being done wherever she can. The distinction breaks down, because the teacher in the informal school may well introduce some material or apparatus (in order to begin, for example, a particular stage in the teaching of reading) which at once catches the children's attention; while in the more formal school, the teacher may use a special interest, which becomes evident, as part of the planned work (for example, when each child makes his own book about something he chooses to write and illustrate). Another difference is often that, in the informal school, the teacher and children work through an integrated day, when there are no special times set on one side for work in a particular field of learning, whereas in the more formal school the morning before 'break' might be devoted to reading, the time after it to number work, and so on. Again, rigid lines of demarcation break down, because in the informal school there sometimes have to be set times when particular groups use some part of the building (often the hall) or when another teacher with special gifts (eg in music) takes them for a period; whereas in the more formal school there may be periods of undirected activity.

The important point for the beginner to realize is that *both* kinds of school have advantages, and in both the teacher is responsible for planning the children's learning. She does this partly by planning the school and class environment and partly by specific teaching, and whether this is done incidentally or in a more systematic way, it has to be done according to a plan.

Generally speaking, the freer the children are going to be, the more carefully the teacher has to plan, keeping records of what is happening, so that she knows exactly what progress each child is making and what help she needs to give him so that he may learn.

Children have already learned more in the five years before they come to school than they are ever likely to learn in such a short time again, and among other things they have learned to use words: they have learned a language. Some of them will have learned this more effectively than others, but they will all have some understanding of the use of words. Even if a child speaks a foreign language, he has still learned what language is. The climate to be established is a climate of literacy rather than a climate of reading, because listening, speaking, reading and writing all go together in learning to read, and although it is sometimes useful to separate them it is wise to remember how closely they are linked.

Our understanding of words is based on experience: in learning to speak, the experience comes first and the word or sentence is attached to it. Unless you have the necessary experience, a word has no meaning for you: it is simply an empty sound. A person blind from birth can never fully understand what is meant by the name of a colour, though he may still give it some meaning in terms of his own experience, like the blind man who said that he thought red must be very like the sound of the trumpet.

When a child first comes to school today, he enters in many infant schools an environment which has been carefully planned, but which he can freely explore within certain limits, in which he can gain experience and in which he is encouraged to talk about what he does. Areas of the classroom are given over to various kinds of experience: to play with water, with sand, with clay, plasticine, dough and similar materials; to constructive play (or 'work' for the two are not divided by young children) with bricks or with junk materials which can be stuck together to make all kinds of things, from trains to houses, and which may include a work-bench with a hammer and nails and odd lengths of wood; to an area where painting and the making of pictures goes on; to a place where there are dressing up materials for all kinds of imaginative play, and where there may be some structure representing a house or a shop; to an area of discovery where he can look at living things (for this includes the nature table), but where there may also be such things as old locks and clocks to be investigated; to an area where things can be sorted according to shape, size, or some other characteristic, counted, weighed or measured, providing some background experience for number work; to an area devoted to books—a book corner, perhaps, where he can look at books, and later read them, without being disturbed by other children, and to which he may later contribute a book of his own, made by himself.

The teacher's first responsibility in this environment (first in time—this is not an order of priorities) is to plan the layout of the classroom and organize the materials so that a learning situation is there and everything necessary is available to the children; then to help the children to learn to use the materials, to explore and discover, to handle what they need and take care of things and put them away when necessary; and then to develop and extend what the children are doing, so that they learn as much as they are capable of learning. The children may choose which area they work in to begin with, though their choice is inevitably circumscribed by the needs and choices of other children. (It helps to establish a background of order if the teacher and children decide together at the beginning how many children can work in each area, and if the teacher then sees to it that the agreed number is not exceeded.) The teacher notices and records what the children do, and sometimes sees to it that they become involved in a new area, which they had not explored before. She also takes groups of children herself for short periods, working with them and teaching them, helping them to learn skills.

The work going on all over the room is part of the climate of literacy. Even playing in the sand, or with water, gives children the opportunity to learn new words, based on immediate experience: light, heavy, soft, dry, pour, castle, heap—all kinds of words may be introduced by the teacher in the course of the children's play, and the children understand them and add them to their vocabulary because they are directly related to what they are doing.

There will be labels to be written and read, pictures to be put up and sentences to be printed in connection with the work and play going on in most of the areas of the room, but the one most obviously connected directly with reading is, of course, the book corner. There should be a shelf of books used primarily by the teacher—books of stories and poetry which she will read to the children, which it is useful to have to hand, so that they can be referred to if an occasion arises, as well as for planned periods of reading; there will be books the teacher may use for reference, too. The children can look at all these, but most of the corner will be arranged to display the books which are especially for the children. To begin with, these will be chiefly picture books, both of information (a simple bird book, for example, or a book of cars) and stories. Having planned an attractive and functional book corner, it is the teacher's responsibility to help the children to use it effectively: to make sure that really interesting, suitable books are there, and that these are changed and added to according to need, and to encourage the children to look at them by reading books to them and suggesting others which may be of special interest.

She needs to note which children use the corner and which need encouragement to do so. A part of every day should be set aside for telling or reading a story or poem, or some factual information connected with the children's other interests, and sometimes the teacher will use a book from the children's part of the library corner, and replace it afterwards for them to look at later. A school library is important, but it is no substitute for this close connection between books and children: the books need to be there in the classroom, so that the teacher can refer to them and use them as opportunity offers during the day. Sometimes the opportunity will have been foreseen and planned, but sometimes it may arise spontaneously: if a child asks a question, or brings something to school, it is a valuable experience for him to see his teacher turn to a book for an answer or illustration, or for further information.

After she has read a story to the children from a library-corner book, the teacher may sometimes produce large pictures of the characters or incidents in the story, or the children may paint these freely for themselves. If the pictures are discussed, and a caption chosen for them, they can be put up on the wall. The children learn that a sentence or a phrase is made up of separate words; they learn what is meant by 'word' and perhaps by 'letters'. They learn through their experience of being read to what reading is, *and what books are*. One cannot assume that all young children will know and understand these words when they first come to school. To decide with the teacher on the best caption, and watch her write it underneath, is in itself an experience in reading. This is the natural way for children to learn that writing goes from left to right, and that this is the way the sequence of words is read. A child becomes familiar with the shape of the words being used, and he can 'read' the final sentence, because he has helped to make it, and knows what it says. In the course of discussion, the children may learn the meaning of some words which are new to them—'wolf', for example, or 'pond'. They gain experience in listening to others and in putting their own ideas into words—all of this is important as a background to reading. Eventually a whole story* may be pinned up on the wall in a series of pictures with captions printed below, which the children can 'read' because they know it. At the same time, they may begin to recognize some words which have been repeated a number of times.

The Advantages and the Special Responsibilities of Teaching Reading in an Informal Environment

Advantages

In a well planned informal environment, the children are constructively occupied: they are actively learning. They may be painting or constructing something, playing with bricks or sand or water, dressing up, reading books, looking at pictures, weighing and measuring, but, if the environment is continuously planned for the children's learning (for the environment is not something static, to be provided and left unchanged), then the chances are that the children working and playing in it are learning all the time. They may not always be learning the 3Rs, but at this stage, from the point of view of

---

* I should like to enter a protest about the use of the word 'story' to mean 'caption', or even 'word under a picture'. The practice is widespread in North America and occurs in Britain too. The effect of such usage is to drain the word 'story' of all its magic and most of its meaning. In this book, I use it only to mean 'a tale that is told'—or written.

learning to read, much of their time may be spent in occupations which encourage them to put their ideas into words, and they learn the meanings of new words by attaching these to experiences as they occur and the teacher, or a more able or older child, comments upon them. They are learning, too, the meaning and purpose of reading. It is not an isolated activity, but a part of their lives.

If they spend time in imaginative play, whether dressing up themselves or playing with bricks or dolls or toys, they are building up imaginary worlds. (The way in which this kind of experience may lead on to reading is discussed later.) They are learning to put themselves into another person's place, seeing the world to some extent through their eyes, getting the feel of what it is like to be someone else. This is an ability which they will need to develop, if they are to get the most out of stories.

If the children are making something, they are learning incidentally to undertake a task, and carry it through to a conclusion: this is something they need to learn, before they can effectively undertake tasks connected with learning skills.

In a well planned environment, much of what the children do is part of the background of learning to read. The informal school does not differ from the more formal one in what it sets out to do, but rather in the way it is attempting to do it, and in the emphasis placed on different aspects of learning.

The teacher has many opportunities for observing the individual children closely in different situations, and of estimating their level of development and when they are ready to learn skills (including reading) in a systematic way. (By 'ready to learn' is not here meant 'when a child wants to learn to read', though readiness may include this, but *when he is capable of learning*. The teacher's task here is not one of passive waiting until a child is ready, but of organizing the learning environment and teaching him in preparation for systematic learning.) There are opportunities, too, for the teacher to note and develop any special interests a child may have, and use these as a basis, perhaps, for his first books.

There is no abrupt change from one level of learning and achievement to another. Children who are slower than others to begin the 3Rs are not conspicuous. Since children are human beings, and we live in a competitive society, those who succeed will sometimes compare themselves with those who don't and exult in their own competence, but those who are not yet able to make a start with books have at least many other constructive things to do which help to prepare them for learning to read.

Problems and Responsibilities

The main problem for the teacher is to make sure that systematic teaching and learning of skills does take place, that there is sufficient practice to reinforce learning, and that no important step or section is left out. When they begin to learn to read, the children must be heard and taught regularly, and this has to be planned as part of each day's work for the teacher.

Children need a stable and secure framework as a background to their lives. There has to be a shape, even to the integrated day. There must be times when something occurs regularly, eg a story-time, when the teacher reads or tells stories to the whole group, a time for music and songs and poetry, a time when quieter occupations are followed and the teacher takes groups and individual children for specific teaching in reading: one cannot teach a group to read against a background of noise, though a quiet hum of activity may be acceptable.

It is important for the beginner to remember that a teacher has as much teaching to do in an informal as in a formal school; it is just that she does it in a different way. But if the children's experiences are to have full value, the teacher must play her part. For example, children will learn a good deal, and may produce interesting pictures, if they are given paints and paper and left free to paint: but they will get much more from the experience if the teacher can sometimes discuss their paintings with them, and if a group of children can sometimes look at the pictures together with the teacher, if she introduces them to different textures, perhaps, and together they notice particularly interesting or lovely patches of colour and design. The danger for the beginning teacher is that the time for this will not be planned and so may be missed, though the experienced teacher, knowing its value, will seize the moment when it is specially relevant. In the same way, in teaching the children to read, there may be a danger for the beginner, in that she is so absorbed by the problem of hearing all the children read as often as possible, that she does not plan the kind of introductory and background teaching which would make a reading series more meaningful.

It is absolutely vital for the teacher to find time to make and keep records of work done by individual children and of their progress and special needs and difficulties.

She must also have a clear plan of the experiences the children should have, the skills they should learn, and the sequence to be followed. In reading, she must know which children have reached the point when specific teaching is necessary, which printed words each child understands and can recognize (his sight vocabulary), when each child is ready to learn skills of word attack (phonics, for example, or the ability to try to work out the meaning of a word from its context); later, which books each child has read and his general level of reading ability; which child needs special help and encouragement.

Establishing a Climate of Literacy in the more formal School Environment

In the more formal school environment, the eventual goal of the teaching of reading is the same: that children shall learn to read fluently and effectively, turning readily to books for information, ideas and experience. But the paths to the goal are more systematically planned and teacher-directed.

The essential background to reading has to be created. There must be opportunities for the children to use spoken language, to learn to put their ideas and feelings into words. There may, for example, be a definite period at the beginning of each morning when children announce their news, rather than this being told at any opportune moment in the course of the day, as it would be in a more informal environment. The teacher may make a news-sheet each day, on which she first writes any item which is of general interest, and later children who are able to do so write their own. The danger is that the news period may become simply a rather dull routine, especially to the children who rarely if ever write any such news; the advantage is that speaking and writing will occur with the whole group every day.

So that the children will see some point in learning to read, apart from the adult approval proficiency brings, the teacher must plan to link reading where possible to something she expects the children will be interested in: a planned school visit, for example, a nature walk or an animal kept in the classroom.

One of the dangers for the beginner to beware of is thinking that if the children are sitting quietly and apparently occupied they are really working, whereas if they are moving about the classroom, using all kinds of materials, they are playing. A child who is painting a picture, or building with bricks, or dressing up, may be learning much more actively than one sitting at a table doing 'seatwork' which consists of colouring in shapes, or underlining letters, but which is not sufficiently interesting or varied to engage his mind and energies.

It is perhaps less difficult to plan to teach reading to groups or individual children regularly every day in the more formal school, but it is just as difficult, perhaps even more difficult, to be sure that the rest of the class is really learning while the teacher's attention is withdrawn.

In a more formal school, it is easier to plan for the systematic and sequential teaching of reading, which is so important; the danger for the beginner is to think that, because something has been taught, it has also been learned. Records of the children's learning, as well as of what the teacher has done, are as important here as they are in an informal school.

It is easier, too, for the beginner to plan periods when stories are read to the children, and perhaps noted or illustrated by them. It is more difficult to be sure that every child is present in mind as well as body while all this takes place, since his body has to be there as part of the group (in an informal school he would probably have more choice of other things to do, so that if he took part, it would be because taking part had value for him).

But in this setting the teacher, and especially the beginner, in planning the week's work, can more easily make sure that nothing important is forgotten, and this in itself can help the inexperienced teacher to feel that she knows where she is, what she has done and what she plans to do. This creates a feeling of confidence and a sense of order in the teacher, which communicates itself to the children, adding to their security.

b IMAGINATIVE EXPERIENCE

The connection between reading and a child's interest in the immediate world about him, in what he is doing or observing at the moment, is only part of the climate of literacy.

The reading of stories to children has already been mentioned as part of the preparation for reading, but it is much more than that: *it is the thesis of this book that stories provide essential imaginative experience, through which we learn about ourselves, about other people and about the world in which we live.*

Books not only record experiences: they widen them. Even in the kind of work suggested already, a book full of the pictures of common birds, with their names printed under them, will have meaning, and the children's experience will be widened just a little, if the book tells them something new about a bird they have seen and directs their attention to other birds, or to bird behaviour, which they would not otherwise have noticed. Even giving a name to something or some creature helps in classification of experience, and is one of the ways in which the thought of past generations is handed on to us. A book about something in which a child is interested widens his experience, and a book which attracts him by its illustrations may introduce a new interest.

But stories have something more to offer: the widening and deepening of understanding of ourselves and the world about us which comes through a sensitive and imaginative response to a tale that is read or told. This is surely one of the most important and rewarding aspects of reading, and if we can help children to discover this kind of experience in books, they will have a reason for turning to them for the rest of their lives. Not only this. Such widening and deepening of experience, with the growth in imagination that goes with it, is important for the whole growth of our understanding.

It is a way of helping us to understand others: to get inside them and imaginatively see the world through their eyes; to develop, as we grow older, compassion and sensitivity to their needs. This kind of experience is obviously of the greatest importance to children, and though no one would expect them to be able to do this at the age of five or six in the way in which they are able to later, we can nourish the beginnings. Wallace Hildick goes even further than this, saying that children's stories are 'of paramount importance in the whole educative and civilizing process of the powers of imaginative and speculative projection: powers that are applicable to the best work in science and mathematics as they are to politics, history and other more "literary" subjects ...'.

We can help children towards an understanding of people from other countries, and of races other than their own, if we include at this stage folk tales and fairy tales from other lands in the stories we read to them and which they may sometimes act afterwards. They will see pictures of heroes who belong to other races, but the stories have much more to offer than this. Folk tales are part of a way of life. They show how the people who told them and handed them on through the generations interpreted the world around them, how they thought and felt. They are part of the culture and background of a people. A shared experience, even of folk tales and fairy tales, and all the imaginative play and interpretation which can go with them, helps to build a common background among different groups.

The attitudes we develop when young are very lasting. In a sense it is not true to say that we have only one life to live: we can enter imaginatively into many lives. We are helped to interpret and understand our own thoughts and feelings and we learn that we are not alone. The barrier between people is broken down. Stories are one of the most ancient ways of teaching; not only stories which are directly didactic (these often fail in their purpose if it is too obvious) but ones which increase our experience through imagination.

Of course, not all stories will be on this level, particularly those which children read for themselves. There is also a place for a tale which amuses or distracts us, or provides us with an opportunity to rest from problems which beset us in the everyday world. Perhaps this is one of the reasons why children sometimes read books which seem to adults to have little real value; it may be one reason for the popularity among adults of detective stories and other ephemeral literature. Each one of us reads at very different levels at different times.

The reading aloud of stories to children will be a very important part of the creation of a climate of literacy. It should be a planned part of every school day. Sometimes the books will be from the school or public library and will be books the children could not read for themselves, but sometimes they will come from the children's own library corner, so that they can look at them afterwards, and know that books and stories are an accessible part of their environment. Since there is likely to be a wide range of reading ability in any class, even among the youngest children in school there may be two or three who can later read the story they have heard, and everyone can look at the pictures. In any case, they will ask for their favourite stories again and again and will soon know some of them by heart.

Terence Lee, writing in the *Proceedings of the UK Reading*

Association, ends his paper with these words: 'to read is merely to reproduce; to write is to create.' Nothing surely can be further from the truth of our experience. When we read or listen to a story, we interpret it all the time in our own terms; we draw on all the visual experience we have ever had to create the scene and people it with characters; we interpret their feelings and response to the situation in which they find themselves only because we can draw on our own past experiences. Each of us inevitably provides his own inner version of the story. Any writer will tell you what a shock it can be to see an artist's illustrations of characters he has created, and it is only when there is some such overt response to writing that we can see how different are the interpretations, the imaginary worlds, created by the same words for different readers. We should think of listening to and later reading stories as intensely active occupations; activity of mind is even more important than activity of body.

We underestimate children if we think that they cannot respond in this way to stories which are within their compass, and we should not insult them by assuming that this is limited to the trite and trivial. Their response will be bounded by their experience, but that experience is by no means always the superficial happiness of the themes of some children's stories, and learning to respond imaginatively is an important part of learning, and as such the proper business of the school.

What kind of stories should we read to the children? We can soon discover experimentally the ones they want to hear again and again, and we have only to watch them at play to realize that their world is not always one of 'sweetness and light'.

I remember a boy of six during the last war, who had come to a school in a safe area from London, where he had been living in a street which had just been half demolished by a bomb. His own home had been damaged and some of his friends had been killed. For the first six weeks in his new school, he spent much of his time playing with a piece of Montessori apparatus. It was a long rectangle of wood, with a series of cylindrical holes in it, arranged in ascending sizes. A number of wooden cylinders, with little brass knobs on them so that they could easily be picked up, fitted into the holes. The child was supposed by Madam Montessori to look at them, estimate the size, and fit each cylinder into the appropriate hole. For this boy, this piece of apparatus became a bomber. With all the cylinders in, it zoomed along in his hands, and then was suddenly turned over, so that all the 'bombs' (the wooden cylinders) fell out together on whatever might be below—the floor, the table, or even a house built with bricks. His drawings and paintings at this time also reflected the grimmer side of the war. A story about a happy little family to whom nothing much ever happened would scarcely reflect this child's experience, or suggest that books had much to offer, unless he wanted a total escape into an unreal dream, and being a normal and fundamentally healthy little boy, he did not seem to want that—he tried instead to come to terms with the experience. It is true, of course, that bombs are no longer a part of most children's lives, but this does not mean that they have nothing to come to terms with. They may have come to school straight from a quarrel between their parents, or have left behind them a younger brother or sister who seems to have taken most of their parents' attention: at least they have to come away and leave him or her in undisputed possession of the home until after school. Children have many adjustments to make: to their own feelings as well as to things which happen. More of them than we sometimes realize have experienced the loss of a relative or a friend—or of a pet animal, which, to a child, had all the attributes of a living human being. They may have been frightened or made unhappy by other children (the idea that young children are 'sweet' and behave sweetly to each other is an adult fiction). They may have come from another country, or another school or town, leaving friends and a familiar environment behind them. Adjustment may not be easy.

This does not mean, of course, that the stories we read to a child should present him with an unhappy world, full of hate and destruction; the young child needs the security of a world in which right triumphs, in which he can feel reassured, in which good predominates, but he needs to find sometimes in stories figures on whom he can project his aggression, his hates and his fears, and people and situations which are at least as varied and interesting as those he creates himself in his play.

Perhaps this is the reason why fairy tales and folk tales are so well liked, and have survived: they recognize that evil and unhappiness exist, but in them good always triumphs, and what is more, it is usually the weak and small who triumph in the end, so that a child can readily identify himself with the unlikely hero, the third son, the ugly duckling.

The point is that we should not underestimate the thoughts

and feelings which children bring to the creation of imaginary worlds.

Since to begin with children cannot read stories for themselves, the teacher must read them aloud as well as she possibly can, taking the character parts and half-acting them, perhaps, as she does so. This is not something to be discontinued as soon as a child can struggle through a book for himself. We learn a great deal about reading, as well as gaining an understanding of the text, by listening to a book read aloud really well. It is something which should continue throughout a child's school life.

NOTES ON BOOKS FOR FURTHER READING

Success and Failure in Learning to Read by Ronald Morris (1965). London: Oldbourne. Revised edition Penguin, 1973. This is one of the most interesting and stimulating books on reading to have been written during the last decade. It provides an essential background of understanding against which other books on specific aspects of reading and on methods of teaching may be set. In it, Morris describes what he means by 'responsive reading', a concept which is important in evaluating the day to day work of the classroom.

Reading in the Modern Infants' School by Nora L Goddard (1958). Published in Unibooks with amendments and additional material by ULP for the United Kingdom Reading Association, 1971. Nora Goddard clearly explains the place of reading in an infant school environment. It is a helpful book for anyone responsible for teaching reading in an informal school, or indeed in a more formal one. (Parents or teachers who are unaware of the thought, planning and specific teaching of reading which occurs in modern infant schools should also read it carefully.) There are detailed descriptions of how a teacher may take a group of children for 'reading', and of useful apparatus, which are especially helpful to the beginner.

The Integrated day in the Primary School is an account by two teachers, M. Brown and N. Precious, of how this was planned in their own school.

PART TWO

Systematic Teaching

2

Written language as recorded speech and the child's own book

It is against a rich background of experience through play and investigation, listening and exploring that the systematic teaching of reading takes place.

The child's own book is a useful means of making the transition from books as something read aloud by an adult to books as something the child can read for himself.

It is a very natural step for a group of children, working with the teacher, to go on from the earlier news-sheets they have made together, and the captions they have printed under pictures the children have painted, to make a book. The words and sentences used in the news-sheets are those suggested by the children. They are printed by the teacher, who records what the children say. She probably guides the children in selecting which sentences are to be recorded, implicitly if not explicitly, but even so they may fairly be described as recorded speech. The sentences in the books the children and teacher make together are of a similar nature.

The book may be about anything which interests the group as a whole, and which concerns something they are doing at the moment: setting up a shop in the classroom, looking after pets, visiting the local post office. To begin with the step may be a very small one: each child in a group agrees to draw or paint a picture of some stage of what the group is doing on a piece of unlined paper of a given size. Captions are written underneath the pictures and the whole combined in a sequence and stapled together to make a book.

Alternatively, or as well as this, each child is asked to make his own book, perhaps about his own family. The children draw the pictures, and captions are written underneath. The children tell the teacher what to write, and captions may then be printed by the teacher faintly in the book. The children print over them, or, when they are able to do so, the teacher will print the captions on a separate piece of paper, and the children copy them. Later, they will print their own.

Such books are often factual ones, but they need not be. No matter how informal the school, the suggestion that they should make a book almost invariably comes, directly or indirectly, from the teacher, and if the teacher is concerned to link reading with imagination as well as with the recording of fact, some of the books can be story books. They may retell a well-known story, which the children have heard and acted and perhaps illustrated many times, or among some groups there are children who will make up stories of their own. At first, the teacher, having a period during the day when she reads a story, chooses one the children like and ask for often. Then she does her best to prepare a wall story—a set of pictures depicting the main events. It is much easier to prepare a wall story if one can draw; but even those who find drawing difficult can perhaps copy pictures from a book, or simply produce scenes with stylized pin men etc, suitably and colourfully clad. These pictures are pinned up in sequence on the wall. The teacher and children together decide on the appropriate caption for each picture. The teacher then prints this on card, and it is pinned up on the wall below the pictures. The teacher can plan specific teaching in connection with wall pictures and captions of this kind, whether they are factual statements or fictional stories.

To print the caption, she should pin a piece of blank card or thick paper of suitable size under the picture, and let the children watch while she prints the words, so that the left to right direction of reading is emphasized, saying the words as she prints them and sometimes emphasizing sounds so that the connection between the written symbols and the spoken word is implicitly underlined, though probably not made explicit at this stage.* The children are likely to look at the pictures and the words themselves in the days that follow, and the teacher may direct their attention to the captions by taking them down, mixing them up, and asking a child if he can put them back under the right pictures. The fact that he does so does not, of course, mean that he can read the words: he may recognize a caption merely because it is longer than the others, because it has an odd corner, or for some such reason, but the teacher should direct the children's attention to the words: for example, by pointing to a word in one caption and asking them if they can find it in others, or asking them to point out any words they know, or the names of characters.

* See Chapter 4

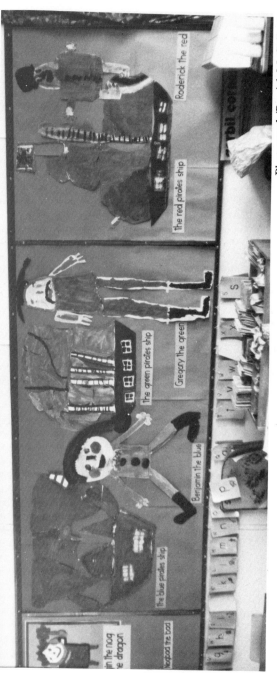

Characters from the stories in their readers which have been painted and cut out by the children

This display serves several functions. The children have interpreted the characters in their own terms, visualizing them, thinking and talking about them and so making them a part of their own imaginative experience. The teacher has seized the opportunity to add the printed names. The children are likely to find their own paintings even more satisfactory than those which might have been drawn by the teacher, and the reading associated with the display becomes part of an interesting activity and part of the children's achievement.

Photograph/Patrick McCullagh

Plate 2

A 'long story' is read to a child, and he then reads it for himself in a book which re-tells the same story in pictures and simple captions.

A page of the child's version:

Mr. Buffins sat down.

The equivalent text in the 'long story' read to the child is as follows:

The dog . . . banged right into the back of Mr. Buffins' legs.
Mr. Buffins sat down. 'Oh!' said Mr. Buffins. 'Woof!' said the dog,
as Mr. Buffins landed on him, knocking all the breath out of his body.

Several wall stories may be used in this way, with the teacher including the same words in captions as frequently as she can. (Making these is time consuming and the stories must be changed frequently, but the pictures can be kept from year to year.) Then comes the point when a group of children make the illustrations for a story, each child depicting one character or episode, and the whole group devising the captions with the teacher as before. Finally, the children make their own books which may tell a story or be about something which interests them (this includes anything from dinosaurs to aeroplanes), which are stapled together and may perhaps be put in the library corner, or sometimes taken home.

The wall story may also be used to lead directly to the making of kangaroo books for the children. These are clearly described by Ronald Morris. Briefly, they are made by taking a story book which children enjoy, where the story is depicted in the illustrations as well as the words, and adding captions to the pictures which are simple enough for the children to read. This can be done by taking the book to pieces and interleaving it with plain paper on which the new captions are printed, or by inserting a short booklet telling the story in simple words in a pocket stuck into the inside cover. (Hence the name 'kangaroo book'.) In making such a book, the same word is often used a number of times, eg *my* book, *my* dog. The child begins to recognize it in new captions. This is a very useful way of becoming familiar with key words—the words used most frequently in all speech and printed material. Murray and McNally claim that twelve words form one quarter of all words read: *a and he I in is it of that the to was.* The problem about these words is that they are not nouns and so can be illustrated only with difficulty. It is not easy to attach them to a concept and not all of them are phonically regular. Still, we are bound to meet them frequently whatever text we write or read and probably the easiest way to learn them is to meet them in context, though the teacher may decide to include them individually later in games as well.

An advantage of the books made by the children themselves is that they can be the child's own recorded speech. They are in fact the only books which can use the spoken vocabulary of each individual child. But here the teacher comes up against something of a problem. We want to encourage children to talk, to be able to put their thoughts and feelings into words, to listen to others with understanding; as teachers of literacy, when the children can handle spoken language with reasonable fluency, we want them to learn to record their thoughts and to read printed language. But the two languages are rarely the same. What they read in printed books is not their own recorded speech: it is, by and large, standard English. For virtually all children there is a good deal of difference between their own speech and the printed word; for some children, the variation is a considerable one. Even if we speak, or think we speak, standard English ourselves, there is some difference for us all, adults as well as children, between the spoken and the printed word. Any child who comes from a home or an area in which there is a strong regional speech which differs in many ways from standard English in pronunciation or structure (or perhaps in both), is faced with two languages at school: the language of books and printed material, which is probably fairly close to the spoken language of the teacher, and his own. There is not just one language of spoken English: there are many variations. (Children from some overseas areas living in this country are often faced with just this problem.)

Now a child's use of words is part of himself. When he first goes to school, he needs to feel that he is accepted as a valuable member of the community in which he finds himself. The feeling of acceptance, of belonging, of human worth, is more important than grammatically correct speech, even if the teacher is considering only the child's success in learning to read, whereas there is in fact much more at stake than this. So in developing a climate of literacy and in helping the child to write his own books a teacher will do well to consider very carefully before she says anything to suggest that a child's usual speech is unacceptable, at least until she has built up a sufficiently happy and confident relationship with him, so that he knows she is helping him to learn, and so that he does not interpret her teaching as a criticism of himself or his home.

At the same time, the teacher has another responsibility towards children (and their parents) and herein lies the problem: books are written, by and large, in standard English; speech which is fairly close to one of the accepted variations of it is an advantage in learning reading skills, eg phonics. It is an important factor in the child's ability to profit by further education. In looking forward to later years, a knowledge of standard English as spoken in the country in which he is living (eg in Britain, Australia, or the USA vocabulary, sentence structure and pronunciation often vary quite considerably) will give a child greater freedom to do what he wants to do. Teachers have a responsibility to see that by the time children leave school they can express themselves fluently and well, and that their speech will not limit them in what they want to do in life. The first aim will not be met if a rigid dull conformity is imposed on them: their speech must always be *theirs*, with its own individual way of expressing thoughts and ideas; but it should also be an effective way of communicating with others.

Perhaps the answer to the problem lies in the teacher's attitude towards human beings and in her sensitivity towards their feelings. The children's own use of words should surely be accepted in the first years of school life, the children being encouraged to make themselves understood and to speak as clearly as they can. At the same time, as they listen to stories being read and to the speech of other people, they can gradually become bilingual, if the language of their home varies much from that of school. This may be the happiest solution, especially if it can occur without the children feeling that one way of speech is better than the other—better in the wrong sense—and without the kind of criticism which checks ease and fluency. What it really means is that the child extends his ability to use the language in new ways, which will serve his needs in all the varying circumstances of his life.

Most homes now have radio and TV, so the children become accustomed to many different ways of speech without consciously considering the matter. Fortunately many of the best-loved characters on the air are people with a very individual way of speaking which adds to their personality. A wide variation is therefore clearly seen to be acceptable.

Later on, when they are older and study English and perhaps foreign languages, the children can learn more consciously what standard English means, but even then a respect for an individual way of using words, as distinct from slovenly speech, is to be encouraged. Poets and writers often use words in an individual and special way, and so enrich the language for the rest of us, and individual and regional variations add colour to the whole.

The more English becomes a world language, the more it will develop local variations. American has diverged widely enough to be given a name as a recognizably different language; anyone living in India or Australia will realize that the English language is growing and developing, shaped by the needs and experience and practice of different peoples. This means that English is a living language, capable of development, but it also means that if one goes to live in a country which speaks a variation of English widely different from one's own, one has to become to some extent bilingual, and this may in some ways be more difficult for the individual to accept than it would be if the language spoken were wholly different—a recognizably foreign language.

In teaching standard English at any level, we are setting out to help children to use words more effectively, and we want to teach grammatically correct written and spoken English as a useful and liberating, not as an inhibiting, means of communication.

Where there are special classes for children who already speak a variation of English as their mother tongue, it may encourage the immigrant children to accept help if there are English children in the same group, and as all teachers know, there are many children native to this country in need of special help in speaking and writing English.

For children for whom English is a foreign language, the situation is rather different. English is so essential to their learning and to their being able to take a full part in the life of the community, that special arrangements have to be made for teaching them. This is particularly important where there are a number of children who speak a foreign language: where there are only one or two children, they are more likely to absorb English from their fellows. As the report on *Organization in Multiracial Schools** indicates, the problem here is that such special teaching needs to be carried on beyond the point when the children can communicate on a basis of simple everyday needs, if they are to profit by an education and books in the English lanuage.

Some teachers use books and captioned pictures made by children themselves as reading material, rather than the first books of a published reading scheme. The advantages are that if the child dictates the contents, the books are written in words which are part of the individual child's own speaking vocabulary and based on his immediate experience and interests. This advantage may outweigh all the difficulties if the particular child or group of children has a very unusual background, one so different from other children in the general population, that there is no reading scheme which is based on

* By H E R Townsend and E M Brittan

background experience he can recognize or imaginatively enter into. But it raises a number of problems, if teacher-and-child-made books are wholly to replace a printed, graded reading scheme.

To begin with, it means a tremendous amount of work for the teacher. If the vocabulary burden (ie the rate of introduction of new words to known words) is to be kept sufficiently low, the teacher has virtually to make a graded reading scheme for each child, or at least for the particular group of children. It is a major task to ensure that the necessary reading skills are taught and the children's interest maintained and to arrange for adequate illustrations. It is possible to teach children to read using a mixture of their own books and kangaroo books, but it needs a skilled and experienced teacher, who has used reading schemes and is prepared to spend a great deal of time making one, to be successful. Further, many children regard printed books as the only 'real' books. So that, except in very unusual circumstances, most teachers, and especially those teaching reading for the first time, find it worthwhile from their own point of view and the children's to introduce and follow at least one published scheme.

NOTES ON BOOKS FOR FURTHER READING

Teachers of immigrant children should read the report already mentioned, *Organization in Multiracial Schools* by Townsend and Brittan, published by the National Foundation for Educational Research, 1972. It encourages awareness of the problems from the point of view of both the teachers and the children and their families and records solutions which have been tried in the schools. The comments of the teachers included in the report are illuminating and helpful to others.

A Wedding Man is Nicer than Cats, Miss, by Rachel Scott, is a personal account of how teachers whose special job it was to teach new immigrant children carried out their work. It is an entertaining book, full of insights and understanding, of useful suggestions and descriptions of work done. This kind of anecdotal account, which is none-the-less firmly based on educational principles and rooted in experience, can be very enlightening. Another interesting account of her work by a teacher of a group of children whose background was unusual (in this instance, Maori children) will be found in *Teacher*, by Sylvia Ashton-Warner.

3

Introducing a published reading scheme

The great advantage of a published reading scheme is that it provides the teacher with books and materials which have been specifically designed and graded to carry the children through the early stages of learning to read. All the work of planning the introduction of new words and the repetition of old ones, the contextual clues to the meanings of words, the placing of words to draw a child's attention to the connection between the printed symbol and the spoken sound, the gradually increasing length and difficulty of the sentences, all this has already been done. Illustrations enrich and give visual clues to the meaning of the text. A reading scheme also provides a framework for a planned approach, particularly if the teacher's manual is carefully studied, and in this way can be specially useful to the less experienced teacher. The reading scheme cannot by itself teach the children to read, but it provides the teacher with the graded books (and usually with at least some of the apparatus) which she needs as an essential part of her own plan.

But in introducing a published reading scheme, there are two problems the teacher must consider. The first problem is concerned with the content of the books, and the second with the inevitable limitations of vocabulary, especially in the very first readers and pre-readers.

a CONTENT

Whatever the reading scheme chosen, the content of the published books cannot, by its very nature, closely match the background of all the children who use them: backgrounds are too varied. Two children living in the same area may come from very different homes, and it is the immediate environment of his home, and perhaps his street, which provides the young child's experience. The home probably includes TV, but the physical circumstances of his life, and the people who are all-important to him, make up a life which may differ very widely from that of even his next-door neighbour. Reading schemes in current use are often criticized as being middle class, but the happy little family they sometimes portray must be as remote from the experience of many middle class children as it is from the experience of any working class child. The background of working class children is equally diverse, and books specially designed for them can only partially reflect their homes. Books in these days have to be published in vast quantities, especially if they are to contain the illustrations which are such an important part of the earliest books a child sees, so that inevitably they cannot be closely linked with the background of the particular group of children reading them, with all its diverse individuals. Further, if we give supposedly middle class children one set of books, and working class children another, this would surely have an unfortunate and divisive effect. (This doesn't mean, of course, that there should not be books with a working class background: we need books with differing backgrounds, and those which reflect the working class setting are valuable because some children may recognize in them likenesses to their own lives, and others may learn to imagine what life is like for people other than themselves.) The point is that we *cannot* provide every child with a published reading scheme which accurately reflects his own familiar circumstances.

The problem is not insoluble; but we have to recognize it, and teach accordingly.

1 To begin with, if children start learning to read with their own books, and with material made or adapted by the teacher to describe all the interesting things which are going on in their own homes and classroom, or which they see outside, which is written in language closely reflecting their vocabulary and speech patterns, then the very first sentences they meet will be tailored to their individual experience and spoken vocabulary in a way in which the books of a published reading scheme can never be.

2 Secondly, even the first printed books the children meet should contain themes which the children understand, because they are within a child's experience: it is the situation and feelings of the characters which children recognize and identify with, rather than the physical circumstances of the imaginary world of the stories, so that although books about ordinary children in familiar settings have value, so have fairy stories and folk tales. Indeed, because a fairy story deals with a situation which a child recognizes as his own—the small weak creature who succeeds in the end, the youngest son who nevertheless triumphs—it may mean more to him and be closer to his own experience and feelings, than a story about a happy little boy and girl who always play together in never-ending sunshine.

Nancy Larrick put the problem clearly in her paper to the United Kingdom Reading Association when she said 'Through one of the most peculiar quirks in the history of education, children's literature is often separated from the teaching of reading.... All too often we have given children dull and colourless reading matter from which we have taken all the humour and pathos, all the sparkle and imagination. A reading lesson becomes a lifeless exercise in which the child is a mechanical participant, reading in a leaden voice, writing in the limited vocabulary he has been taught to read, and thinking the flat thoughts to which he has been exposed.'

We may feel that the situation described here belongs to the past, rather than the present. Nancy Larrick was speaking from a North American background, but it should be read very thoughtfully by anyone who feels that all would be well with the standards of literacy in our schools if we concentrated on the mechanics of reading. The content of the first books a child meets which he reads for himself is important, because he is having not only to translate written symbols into speech, but is learning what reading is.

J R Tolkien, in his book *Tree and Leaf*, describes how a writer creates a 'Secondary World'. The 'Primary World' is the world you see and experience around you. The 'Secondary World' is the imaginary world created by the writer, into which the reader enters for the duration of the story. It is a measure of the writer's skill that this world should seem real to us while we are in it, and at the simple level of a first reading scheme the words need all the help that illustrations can give, supplemented by any other material which will help a child to re-create this secondary world in his own imagination. But if the story is a good one, even at a very simple level, the 'Secondary World' will in some sense be true to the experience and understanding of the reader of the way in which people behave in his own 'Primary World'. A story can depict many things which are true to life, even though the setting may be based on no known country and the characters may be strange creatures which we see only in pictures.

The same criteria which we apply in choosing the stories we read *to* children should prevail in selecting the first printed story books which the children are being asked to read for themselves. The common elements in the stories should be the experiences of human childhood. Books which deal with these, whether they are about 'real' children or animals and other creatures in an imaginary setting, can have a unifying effect, because through them children from quite different backgrounds can have a common imaginative experience and recognize their own human feelings and predicament.

There is another, more technical reason, why stories with a folk-tale/fairy-tale setting are useful in a child's earliest printed books: they are stories in which there is often a good deal of repetition *as an integral part of the story*, and are told in sentences which contain their own rhythm. This is often true of traditional stories (the folk-tales of the later *Beacon Readers* have this quality) but it can also be part of books specially written for a reading scheme. *Fish and Chips*, in the *Nippers** series, uses a traditional story pattern in modern dress to achieve this effect, and in *The Old Man and the Wind†* an attempt is made to provide such natural rhythmic repetition in a fairy-tale setting:

> The very next day,
> The wind came....
> The wind blew in
> at the window,
> and the wind blew in
> at the door.
> The wind blew and blew and *blew*.

Not only do the children meet the same words again and again, but the momentum of the sentence carries them along. It is all part of the story.

3 When the children are ready to go on to printed books, the teacher can plan the introduction to the reading scheme in such a way that the children as individuals, or as a group, *gain the experience they will need for interpreting the text before they meet the books*, so that when they do read them, the words used are already part of their spoken vocabulary.

* Edited by Leila Berg
† *One, Two, Three and Away!* by Sheila McCullagh

Reading published books, even the simplest of primers, introduces a new stage in learning to read: the book the child made himself, or the teacher made for him, reflected or recorded his own ideas and experience; published books extend that experience, and since this extension of one's own life is one of the reasons for learning to read in the first place, it is something to be encouraged. But the children will only be able to respond to the text if the vocabulary is within their understanding, and the only way a teacher can ensure that, is to see that the children have the necessary experiences and the words to describe them before they meet the books.

Suggestions

(a) The most obvious way of solving the problem is to plan an actual experience. If the first books of a reading scheme are about children visiting a shop or a fire-engine, a post office or a zoo, then a class visit to see the local shop, fire-engine or other setting, provides immediate experience and many opportunities for discussion and for the learning of new words. But although such an expedition may be most valuable on occasion, it is not as simple a solution as it may at first appear to be. To begin with, the range of possible visits is limited: the readers may be based on some background which is out of reach. For example, one version of the *Beacon Readers** begins with stories about Old Lob and his farm animals. For children within the reach of a farm, an actual visit might help, though the animals on Old Lob's farm are closer to folk-tale animals, who speak and act like human beings, than to the ones the children are likely to see on a modern farm. But that approach would not in any case be open to most city children.

A second difficulty is that different books in a series may have different backgrounds, and too many visits, as well as being difficult to arrange, may be very disturbing for the children and the general life of the class. There is a great deal to be said for learning in tranquillity.

A third difficulty is that if the earliest books are based, as so many are, on a home and family background, it is not easy to arrange an actual visit to a home which meets the requirements, and even if it were possible to do so, it might not help very much. Looking on at something is not the same

* J H Fassett

experience as being part of it, and the children's defences are soon aroused if they feel that their own family and its way of life are being criticized, even implicitly. In rejecting what seems to them to be the implied criticism in the books, they may even reject the books themselves and the reading which goes with them.

In the *Dominoes* reading scheme the author, Dorothy Glynn, offers a solution to this problem by basing the books on the school environment. They are about eight children and their teacher in an infant school, and the early books record what the children do. A teacher using this scheme could so shape the environment in her own classroom that it closely resembled that in the books, and the children reading them would be carrying out the same kinds of activities. But the problem here is that the vocabulary built up in the very first books refers to activities in the classroom, and this may limit the possibilities for interesting stories in later books, or alternatively increase their vocabulary burden, since new imaginary worlds have to be described from the beginning.

So that, although actual experiences are useful where they can readily be arranged, it is not possible and perhaps not even wise to rely wholly upon them.

(b) One of the most important ways in which young children gain experience and assimilate ideas is through their play, and this can provide another and very effective solution to the problem. It is also easier for the teacher to arrange as part of the planned approach to reading. When we as adults read a book, we enter in our imagination into a secondary world, the imaginary world created by our response to the words we are reading. Children create such imaginary worlds all the time, long before they can read, in their play. Sometimes they act (or 'live', for they can be totally involved in what they are doing) the lives of the characters themselves, when they pretend to be mothers and fathers, or daleks or Peter Rabbit or the doctor, nurse or coalman, or whoever it may be. Sometimes they create a visible imaginary world with symbols, with toy animals and houses and people. It is not a very big step from the secondary world the child creates in his play to the secondary world built up by the symbols of words, spoken or printed, in a story.

In her book *Reading in the Modern Infants' School*, Nora Goddard describes how the play-house in the classroom became the house of the family met in the early readers, and how the names of the characters were printed on cards, and given to the children to wear as they took the parts of the various people in the stories. They did not necessarily act the stories from the books. They simply played at house, but the house became the one in the text, and as mother, father, or child they assumed the names of the people they were reading about. The children can invent what happenings they like in their play-house, but because the link is made with the books, the content of the first readers has a meaning which might otherwise be lacking and the children incidentally come to recognize the printed names.

In *One, Two, Three and Away!* wooden toy figures of the people in the story are part of the pre-reading materials for the scheme, so that the children can set up a Lilliputian world in which the three families they are going to read about live. The children come to know the 'Story People' and part-fairy-tale/part-realistic setting of the tales, the names of the characters, their homes and the place where they live, and find that the books, when they come to them, are about people they already know. The fact that the *Story People* live in the Village With Three Corners does not mean that the books are designed for country children: it is simply a way of making them part of an imaginary world, a community which is small enough for the children to understand—which is small enough, in fact, to reflect the pattern of their own relationships with parents, friends and other adults. In this series, too, the names of the characters in the stories—the Red-hats, Blue-hats and Yellow-hats—serve two purposes. First, they emphasize the fairy-tale nature of the setting, and thus at the same time *generalize* it, and make it acceptable to children of widely different backgrounds (because the setting is in an imaginary 'secondary' world, and does not pretend to reflect the particular streets in which the children themselves live). Against this setting, the four children who are the main characters in the books, none-the-less encounter the kinds of problems and situations any child can recognize, because although the setting may be different, the problems are ones he encounters in his own life: adults who help him; adults who won't let him do things he wants to do; children who are not invariably happy and kind to others as well as those who are.

Secondly, another purpose of the names is to encourage the children to take the parts of the people themselves in their play. Children like to have some simple property, to dress up, when they are playing. For play in a house, they immerse themselves more happily in the characters of mother and father if they can wear an apron or a scarf (or of course a name card) which they imagine a mother wearing. For children reading the books in *One, Two, Three and Away!* the necessary properties are obvious and simple for the teacher to provide: all that is needed are hats—paper hats if necessary, which the children can make for themselves—coloured red, blue and yellow.

But whether a reading scheme has been specially designed with this kind of approach in mind or not, the children and teacher together can provide a setting in which the children, through their play, use the words in the stories they are going to read, and use them against a background which gives them meaning.

b LINKING SPOKEN AND PRINTED VOCABULARIES

There is another very important reason for spending time on this kind of introduction to the books: it provides an opportunity for the teacher to make sure that the words they will meet in the first printed books they read are part of the children's spoken vocabulary. Speech comes before reading. Developing the children's ability to put their ideas into spoken language is an important part of the background of literacy, and an essential preparation for the teaching of reading. The children will not be able to respond to printed words which mean nothing to them, even if they can translate the printed symbols into sounds.

In his book *The Teaching of Reading*, Donald Moyle cites a research study reported by Vernon (1948). Vernon observed the conversation of 200 children between $4\frac{1}{2}$ and $5\frac{1}{2}$ years old, and recorded the words they used. Donald Moyle continues: 'The astounding result to come from this research was the tremendous variation from one child to another, for among 200 children only 491 words were used in common by 15 or more children. *Thus although children may use quite a large number of words there will be considerable variety concerning which words these are from one child to the next.*' (My italics.)

Donald Moyle's conclusion is that 'the vocabularies of early readers will have to be restricted to a small number of most used words'. But such a solution carries with it its own inherent danger: if we use in the text only words which we are virtually certain all the children meeting the books will already use, the vocabulary becomes so restricted that the content is almost inevitably emasculated and trivial, and so ceases to engage a child's mind and imagination, and perhaps eventually even his attention. There has to be a compromise.

The solution lies partly in the books themselves: they convey information, or the theme of a story, partly by text but partly through pictures, and in the earliest books there is likely to be a very high proportion of illustration. Any word which might be outside the experience of the children should have visual clues to its meaning provided by the pictures. But if we are creating within the classroom play situations which bring the books to life, we already have a useful opportunity for extending the children's vocabulary by introducing into their play the actual words of the text they are going to read. For the teacher, this means a careful study of the books, bearing in mind the particular group of children she is teaching and individual variations within that group. It is useful to make a note of any words likely to be new to the children, so that she can be sure that they meet them in the course of their play, their pre-reading experience. To give a simple example, in book 2 in *One, Two Three and Away!* Billy falls into a duck pond. City children living within reach of a park are likely to know what a duck is, and also what a pond is; children living in the heart of a city, and never moving outside their streets, extend their vocabulary to include such words partly through looking at pictures (not only those in the book, but also by what they see, for example, on. TV), but if they have made their own Village With Three Corners, they will already have set up the houses for the children and their families in the setting, which includes the pond, and the teacher, discussing it with them and perhaps providing a tiny toy duck, will have given them the necessary words to describe it as she talks with the children about the model they make and play with.

It also becomes clear that, when they start reading the books, 'hearing the children read' must often include discussion of the pictures as well as making sure that the children can read the text. The children should already have learned to look at pictures, to understand what is happening in them, to notice the people and to think about what they see; but this pre-reading experience has to be extended and used with the reading series, transferred to the next situation, and of course used with other books which the teacher will be reading to the children as well.

Sentence structures may need introduction as well as individual words. The problem of using the child's own speech has already been discussed. As soon as the children begin using a published reading scheme, they will meet sentences whose structure differs from the ones they use themselves in speech. Printed books cannot reflect the individual speech patterns of every child who reads them, any more than they can accurately reflect his environment, though this does not absolve the writer of such books from providing sentences which can readily be understood and spoken by the children. The writer must also use sentences which flow as naturally as possible, as well as allowing for all the other considerations concerning the introduction and repetition of new words which will make the books effective 'skill-acquiring instruments'. But, with the best will in the world, the books cannot accurately reflect the speech patterns of all the children who will read them.

This is part of learning to read. Very few of us 'talk like a book'. To say that someone 'talks like the encyclopaedia' is a very double-edged compliment. We have different acceptable vocabularies for speaking, reading and writing, and we use differing sentence patterns. So that, in reading a published book, a child enters on a new stage in learning to read, a new facet of the skill. It is the teacher's responsibility to prepare him for it.

She may do this partly by the words she chooses. To give a very simple example, for children using the *Ladybird Key Words Reading Scheme*,* one might have three pictures, one of Peter, one of Jane, and one of the dog. Before the children begin book 2a in which the dog is introduced, she could collect the group of children about to start the book, and hold up the pictures, first of Peter and then of Jane, asking who they are. The children will probably answer with the one word 'Peter' and 'Jane'. The teacher then holds up both pictures, one in each hand, and says, 'Yes: here is Peter and here is Jane' (indicating each by looking at it as she speaks). She then holds up a picture of the red setter, and says, 'And here is Pat, the dog.' She pins up the pictures on the wall, and produces sentences on cards which go underneath: 'Here is Peter; here is Jane; here is Pat, the dog.' What the teacher is really trying to do is to create a setting

* W Murray

Plate 3

Photograph/Patrick McCullagh

Children in a Primary School unpacking a parcel

Parcels are one way of stimulating interest in a topic. Children always find it exciting to open a strange parcel which has come through the post. Here, they are opening the box and discovering the Story People, but a similar parcel might contain many things: for example, pictures and letters sent by children in a country school to those in a city.

Plate 4

Photograph/Lois Myers

Playing with the Story People in the Village With Three Corners

Mrs. Blue-hat and Mrs. Red-hat are having a conversation and the two children are talking through the characters.

in which the sentences from the books take their place as part of ordinary speech.

This brings us to the second problem: how to make the books, and especially the very first readers and pre-readers, interesting reading, with their inevitable limitations of vocabulary.

C OVERCOMING THE RESTRICTIONS OF A LIMITED VOCABULARY

The first problem, then, was to give a group of children experiences in common, which would help them to understand the words and ideas in the particular series they are going to use in learning to read. The second problem is closely linked with it. It is put very clearly by Wallace Hildick: 'Here the books that are to be read by children must be carefully designed and manufactured as precision instruments—skill-acquiring instruments—with strictly limited and graded vocabularies, sentence structures and lengths. That these instruments are usually constructed in fictional form—very simple, bare, gutless narratives—is at once a tribute to fictions' power to attract and engage and a very dangerous hazard: a threat to a child's future capacity to enjoy prose fiction and thereby derive from it the immense educative benefits it has to offer. Indeed, without certain balancing factors, an initial diet of such drab, lifeless, skill-acquiring narratives can completely cancel out the real value of the skill acquired.' Hildick's solution is to make sure that children should, while they are learning to read, be 'systematically regaled and refreshed' by listening to much richer stories, read to them by adults.

The reading of stories aloud by adults is an essential part of the climate of literacy, and the only point which needs to be stressed is that it should continue throughout school life. But the text of the primer itself can be a good deal enriched by a teacher willing to spend thought and imagination on stories directly connected with it. This is really a development of the kangaroo book idea. Just as it is possible to read the children a story and then make a very simplified version of it (perhaps with a few captions) which they can read for themselves, so it is possible to reverse the process, to take the text of a primer and weave an interesting story around it.

This can be done with any text, no matter how banal or arid it appears at first sight. Imagine for a moment that the teacher has read the story of Puss in Boots to the children and that they have enjoyed it, as most children do. Now imagine that she invents a new episode, in which puss encounters a magician who has a flying carpet, a magic mat which would carry anyone stepping on it wherever he wished to go. In such a context, even the simple statement 'The cat sat on the mat' would carry a good deal of meaning and bring forth an imaginative response from the children.

Some reading schemes provide such stories for teachers: the *Queensway Readers*,* for example, provide a book of stories about the family who feature in the first readers, telling of things which happened just before the first book begins—before the children go to school. In the *Griffin Pirate Stories*,† there are stories of the pirates which are recorded on tape, as well as being in the handbook for the teacher to read, which again introduce the main characters and, specifically, the pre-readers—the first books the child will meet in the series. In one story the text of a pre-reader is embedded in the longer story, word for word, as an episode, a part of the whole. But the technique can be used by any teacher, with any reading scheme. Even if the teacher is not usually given to making up stories, she can expand the simple text of a first primer to make it much more interesting than it would be if read or told solely in the words of the text.

This practice may have the additional and perhaps unexpected bonus of making the reading scheme much more interesting to the teacher as well as to the children: it becomes something which engages her own thought and imagination as well as theirs. This is a great advantage, because the teacher who finds the primers interesting, is much more likely to convey that interest to the children she teaches, than one who is bored with them. The importance of the teacher in the reading situation, irrespective of the method she follows, is not to be underestimated.

d ESTABLISHING A BASIC SIGHT VOCABULARY

The next step in teaching the children to read the first books of a reading scheme is to establish a basic sight vocabulary.

* M Brearley and L Neilson
† These are designed for children beginning to learn to read in the junior school, but are sometimes used for younger children as well.

Even if a teacher begins by teaching phonics there will inevitably be some words which the children have to recognize by sight. If the words used in the first books of a reading scheme are to convey interesting ideas, then some of them at least will be too difficult for the children to unlock with the simple phonic skills they are beginning to acquire. Otherwise the text is likely to be as meaningless as that of Sonnensschein's, which (to quote Ronald Morris) 'began with the simple aria "I go so. So I go. No, I go so" and ended with that cheerful invitation to suicide "On a sunny day it is delightful to walk over the chalk cliffs of Dover".'

Even if the teacher is going to follow a new method of decoding, such as *Words in Colour*, or to use a new medium such as i.t.a., it is still important that the children should not have to decode every word, but should recognize an increasing number of words at sight. (Decoding only comes into its own when the reader is faced by a word he does *not* recognize at sight.)

If the teacher is following the general practice of many schools, decoding will come later, and will probably be at least partly taught through words the children already know.

Many of the words he will meet should already be known to the child* at this stage. The names of the characters and their homes should have become familiar through play; many of the key words in the sentences will have been seen, and copied by the children in writing captions for their pictures, and in making their own books.

It is very important that, when a child comes to his first book, he should find that he can read it. Nothing succeeds like success, and such a beginning encourages him and gives him confidence to continue. If the teacher has a list of the words he will meet, she can make sure that most of them at least will be familiar. The illustrations in the book will help the child to recognize other words, particularly if he has already learned to use pictures for visual clues. If wall charts of some of the pages are provided, these are a halfway house to the book. The wall charts may be looked at and read together by the teacher and the group of children about to embark on the book, so that the first page at least is familiar. There is another advantage in a wall chart, too: the teacher can re-emphasize the directional nature of reading by point-

* The singular is used rather than the plural here, but the whole question of individual and group teaching is discussed in Chapter 6.

ing to the beginning of the word or sentence under the picture in the wall chart and moving her finger along from left to right as it is read.

The first books, pre-readers (which may contain captions but are pre-readers in the sense that they precede the main readers) or introductory books, should be very short, so that the success comes quickly.

A very simple procedure may be followed: the teacher takes the child or children who are beginning the book. Together, they look at the pictures and discuss them, and the teacher asks a child to read the captions. According to their progress and ability, and the simplicity of the book, they may read a number of pages together in this way, or even a whole book if the first pre-reader is very short and the children well prepared. (Some pre-readers are only 8 pages long.) If there are any words which a child does not at once recognize, the teacher will help him, perhaps by reading the word for him, perhaps by referring him to the picture. (Teachers who begin by teaching decoding may help the child to decode the word at this point, though most teachers defer decoding to a rather later stage.)

In any case, the session should be a short one, the children should go off to look at their books with a feeling of an adventure successfully accomplished and the teacher should make a brief note of which pages were read and any words a child has not immediately recognized.

At this stage in learning, it is important that the teacher arranges to work with the children who are just beginning 'real' reading every day, so that the next time they come together the pages studied on the previous day may be read through quickly by the individual children, before they go on to the new pages.

It may be that the children will remember the word they did not previously know; but in any case a good deal has to be done *outside the books* to establish the vocabulary. No book could, by itself, provide enough repetitions of words to establish their recognition by the children, and retain much meaning or (a point sometimes forgotten) retain a flow of sentences which are reasonably close to normal speech.

Repetition of the words may sometimes be included in the general activities of the class: eg the teacher might put up a picture relating to some other class interest, and deliberately use the new word as part of the caption, drawing the children's attention to it and reminding them that it is a word they met in their new book; or the teacher might print a sentence on the blackboard before the children come in, telling them something they will want to know (perhaps about a visit, or a pet, or some event in the school), including new words they have met in their books.

The words may be included in captions in the children's own books, or printed by the teacher on cards to be used with the group reading a particular book. If each child is given a card with a word on it, these may be set out in sentences by the children, always beginning on the left and working towards the right, and collected afterwards by asking a child to pick up a card with a certain word on it.

Watching the teacher print a new word in his book or on the board will help a child to learn to recognize it, especially if he is actively looking for clues which will help him remember; printing the word himself from a copy will help too, for then he must pay close attention to the letters; on both occasions the idea of the left to right nature of reading is reinforced.

But in all these learning situations, the attitude of the learner is all-important. A child who is actively trying to remember and learn the words is more likely to be successful than one who has 'turned off', and is thinking about something else; taking time to make learning interesting and letting the children see the purpose of what they are doing is time well spent. So is a knowledge of results. A set of cards labelled 'Words I know' (or 'Words we know') which grows longer every day, can be encouraging to a beginner, and running through them from time to time can provide useful practice and revision.

Some reading schemes provide useful apparatus to help in establishing the basic sight vocabulary, by providing for frequent repetition of words in games, or in a semi-play situation. If such apparatus is available and effective, it should be used at this point, but it is rarely possible for the teacher to manage without making at least some herself, for individual children who need special practice and materials which fit in with her own way of teaching.

In making apparatus (or of course in buying it) it is worthwhile keeping the following points in mind:

(a) It should be effective, ie it should give the children plenty of practice in recognizing words, or in reading, for the amount of time spent. It should be teaching (or reinforcing) word-recognition or reading skills and not simply occupying the children.

(b) It should be reasonably durable but not too durable; apparatus has to be made outside school hours and the amount of time available for making things is limited. On the one hand, the apparatus should stand up to considerable and if possible varied use; on the other, the teacher will probably want to revise and adapt it as time goes on; and generally speaking, it should not take too long to make unless a teacher is sure, from experience, that it will be worthwhile. If too much time is spent, a teacher will have a natural reluctance to scrap apparatus even if it is not really effective.

Word and picture matching cards* are useful, especially for teaching nouns. If the teacher is not able to copy illustrations from the book, and none are supplied with the scheme, then it is worthwhile to take a book to pieces, and mount the pictures on cards for this purpose. The captions which fit under the illustrations are then printed on separate strips of card. Separate word cards, making up the sentences, can be included.

Word-and-picture-matching material can be turned into games. A set of cards with pictures on some cards and matching words on others can be used in a number of ways, eg if two or three children are playing together the whole set may be placed face downwards on the table, and each child in turn picks up a card. If it is a picture-card, he keeps it, placing it face upwards in front of him. If it is a word-card, he looks at the picture-cards he has collected. If it matches one, he keeps it; if it doesn't he returns it face downwards to the table. The object of the game is to collect as many pairs of picture and word cards as possible.

It is useful to make a reference card to accompany such a game, ie a sheet on which the pictures and matching words on the cards are shown in pairs. Each child can use this to make sure that his pairs are correct, so that the game is self-corrective and the children can play independently. Furthermore, reference cards provide useful experience when the teacher and children later make and use picture dictionaries.

It must be remembered that, although the words are met separately in such practice, they were first met in context in the books or in the children's writing. In any study of single

* More detailed suggestions for games will be found in Chapter 6.

words, this background of reference is important. It provides a context which helps the children to understand not only the individual words, but the whole purpose of studying them, and so provides an incentive for them actively to seek to learn.

It will have become clear to the beginner, if she were ever in any doubt on the subject, how important it is for the teacher to know the words which the children will meet in the books, and plan accordingly. They will not need to know every individual new word before they meet it; the pictures and contents of the book will help them to 'read' words they have not met before, and the books themselves will provide for many of these words to be used many times in slightly different contexts. The children may 'read' some books, especially at the beginning, with considerable reliance on the pictures to help them, so that they get the feel of reading a book. But it is nonetheless important for the teacher to keep a record of the sight vocabulary which the children are building, so that she may be able to arrange useful learning situations and where possible anticipate difficulties before they arise.

Someone who has not taught reading before may well feel that she should, to begin with, concentrate on using one main reading scheme, with perhaps others for supplementary reading or for a few children for whom the main scheme seems to be unsatisfactory. She can then adequately prepare the children for it and arrange her teaching accordingly. As she becomes more experienced and more familiar with different reading material, she may wish to introduce a number of schemes. Some experienced teachers build a number of books from different reading schemes together into a plan of their own. But whatever combination of books may be used, the teacher must remain aware of the importance of introducing the children to the books in a context which makes 'real reading' possible—Morris's 'responsive reading'—and which allows her to provide adequate teaching and practice. A beginner (or even a more experienced teacher) should make a reasonable estimate of the time, energy and ability she has, in deciding how many different schemes she will use in planning for the children's learning. But as soon as the child is successfully through the first stages, and is beginning to develop an attack on new and unknown words, a wide variety of carefully graded books for him to choose from, at least as supplementary readers, becomes more and more important, and this is the point where books from a number of reading schemes can most usefully be introduced.

NOTES ON BOOKS FOR FURTHER READING

The Teaching of Reading by Donald Moyle, is a useful general handbook for teachers. It covers a wide range of topics, but there are many detailed, practical suggestions for work in the classroom. It also contains a glossary, which any teacher who has not yet read widely in this field would find particularly helpful, and lists of attainment and diagnostic tests, and of reading schemes.

Children and Learning to Read by Elizabeth J Goodacre, is an excellent book for those who wish to study the relevance of modern research findings to the whole subject. It is essential reading for any teacher setting out to understand the principles underlying different methods of teaching, and the development of understanding and of auditory and visual perception which makes reading possible.

The publications of the *United Kingdom Reading Association* are another source of information about teaching methods and modern research. Many of the papers published are full of stimulating and practical ideas.

Standards and Progress in Reading by Joyce M Morris, also published by UKRA is an important study of an inquiry carried out in the schools in Kent. It is for the student who is willing to undertake a piece of serious study-reading, but it is a most useful source of information which less experienced teachers might consult for particular information. It contains among other things as an appendix *A Review of Recent Research on Reading and Related Topics with a Selected Bibliography*, by B S Cane.

Anyone who would like to see how a particular piece of research can be interpreted to provide insights into teaching methods will find an interesting example of this if she first reads *Learning to Think* a paper by H F Harlow published in *Readings in Educational Psychology* (Methuen, London 1970) and then reads *What Children Learn in Learning to Read* by Ronald Morris, published in *English in Education*, Vol 5, No 3, 1971, and reprinted in the Penguin edition of

Success and Failure in Learning to Read.

READING SCHEMES

A new teacher often has to use whatever books are available, and an inexperienced teacher is usually well-advised to wait for a while before changing to a new reading scheme. But there are many alternatives, and anyone faced with a choice would find Vera Southgate's paper on *The Problem of Selecting an Approach to the Teaching of Reading* helpful. After a brief introduction, it lists points for consideration when examining reading schemes, books and apparatus. It will be found in *The Second International Reading Symposium*, edited by John Downing and Amy L Brown, and has been reprinted in *Beginning Reading*.

Most reading schemes have a handbook. This should be essential basic reading for a teacher using the scheme, not because she is going to follow it slavishly (she may not follow it at all) but because it will provide useful information. Circumstances and children vary, and teachers adapt primers and apparatus freely in planning their work with the children, but if the teacher has read the handbook at least she knows what books and materials are available for any particular scheme, and how they are designed to fit together. (It is as well, too, to check with the publisher of a reading scheme being used in the school to see whether there are any recent additions of books etc.)

Many local authorities, teachers' centres, and university institutes and schools of education provide lists of reading schemes and materials available, and some have collections of text books which may be examined.

An up to date list of *Reading Schemes for Primary Schools* and *Reading Schemes for Slow Learners* is published by the University of Reading *Centre for the Teaching of Reading*.

4

Developing Independence:
the use of Phonics

Most teachers introduce the teaching of phonics into their reading programme at some point, but there is considerable individual variation concerning when and how the connection between grapheme and phoneme, the written symbol and the sound associated with it, is taught. Some people teach this incidentally as the opportunity arises; some teach it very systematically, according to a carefully worked out plan. It is for the individual teacher to decide, because some will find they can teach more effectively in one way and some in another; it is partly a matter of the teacher's own personality, and the method she finds best suited to her own way of teaching, and partly a matter of the children and the general practices of the school. But the following points are worth considering in planning this part of the teaching of reading, and even if phonics are to be taught incidentally, it is helpful for the teacher to have in mind in some detail the aims she is hoping to achieve, the sequence of steps to be followed and the skills she is planning to cultivate.

Skill in 'sounding out' a word is a child's most effective tool for decoding a printed word which he will recognize when it is spoken and alternatively, in his writing, of en-coding, recording his speech. It is interesting that one of the points made strongly by teachers using i.t.a. was that the teacher felt freed from the constant demands from many children who were able to write down their ideas without asking the teacher how to spell every word: i.t.a. provided at least some of them with a method they could understand and use for recording spoken words easily on their own. Another advantage is that a knowledge of phonics makes for a different *kind* of learning. When a child is learning a basic sight vocabulary he is learning to respond to a visual symbol with a spoken word which has meaning for him: we tell him that a printed shape stands for a given word, and he learns to respond with the spoken word. But when we are teaching him phonics, we are teaching him how men may communicate through marks on paper, ie the alphabetic principle underlying the writing of most languages (Chinese is the obvious important exception, but it is interesting that, now that universal literacy is their aim, the Chinese are planning to abandon their traditional writing for an alphabet). We are helping him to *understand what he is doing.*

If he achieves this understanding, another value from such teaching should be the child's growing ability to decode more and more of the words he sees written all around him, printed on packets and displayed in shops when he is out with his mother, as well as in books and papers. This gives him the feeling that he is succeeding—that he is able to read.

But a good deal of all this depends on how and when phonics is introduced and taught. The dangers are as clear as the advantages. It can be a meaningless exercise in which a sound is associated with a letter, or group of letters, by sheer drill, and the children never realize how such sounds fit into words, and never use what little knowledge they have in the reading situation. There is little or no transfer of training from the lesson in phonics to reading a book, because the children have not understood the connection between the two, nor have they been shown how to use their knowledge of phoneme/grapheme relationships to work out an unknown word.

When an understanding of phonics has so many advantages, it is easy to see why some teachers have made it the beginning and central core of their teaching of reading. But to do this brings the disadvantages of a phonic approach clearly to the fore. They are principally these: that it is very difficult indeed (I would say impossible) to write a story or a factual account in English which conveys ideas children would want to decipher, in words which are phonically regular, and moreover in the simple letter/sound relationships children will learn at the beginning. This means that if one *begins* by teaching the letter sounds, or even begins with material which chooses words predominantly because they can be easily decoded by the beginner, one risks the danger Hildick describes of the 'skill-acquiring instruments' being so dull and meaningless that they will put the children off reading for ever. Secondly, the work done in providing a climate of literacy, in the children's own books and the reading material made and used in the general activities of the classroom, inevitably demands the use of sight words: words which, because they could not be sounded out, became known as 'look and say' words. (It will have already become clear that the use of 'look and say' as a term for all visual methods can be very misleading indeed.) Undue concentration on phoneme/grapheme relationship can also cause the 'barking at print' which we are seeking to avoid—the lack of that response to the meaning of words which is of such great importance, and which is an integral and fundamental part of the skill of reading, so that, in learning to call out sounds and words, the children will not be learning to read at all. It is true that there is a point when some children seem temporarily to concentrate so intensely on translating the printed into the spoken word that they are absorbed by this one aspect of the skill. But after they have spoken the words once, their attention can be redirected to the content of their reading. The dangers will be greatest for the children who find reading difficult, because they will remain longest in the early stages.

The value of phonics depends, therefore, on when and how the sound/letter (or groups of letters) relationship is introduced and taught.

a BACKGROUND EXPERIENCE

Many teachers in this country have done their best to combine different methods in teaching children to read. Emphasis on one method or another can be varied according to the age and abilities of the children, and to the ways which prove most effective for the individual teacher concerned.

The approach to reading through the climate of literacy, through the interest of the children and through stories, is also a useful approach to the teaching of phonics. It is an invaluable context within which the teaching of phonics may begin, in which the purpose of phonics is thoroughly understood by the children and in which they learn to use their new skills.

Just as the teaching of reading does not begin with a thunderclap, when a child is shown his first printed word or sentence, but is preceded by a period in which he learns to use words in speech, and to realize what reading is and its value for him, so the teaching of phonics does not begin at the moment when the relationship between letter and sound is apprehended for the first time, although this may be a big step forward.

A child first has to learn to listen, and this is something which can be encouraged quite informally by the teacher from the time he first comes to school—and before then by his parents at home. Listening to birds singing, Concorde going over, the different sounds in the early morning in the city or in the countryside, inside or outside the school, and distinguishing between them, is part of learning to listen. To give a simple example, a child (or the teacher) finds a beetle, and brings it into school for the children to see in a matchbox before letting it go. The children listen to the faint scratching sounds and try to guess what is in the box before it is opened. This is all a part of learning.

Children respond to changes in the sound of voices at a very young age, as every parent and teacher knows: they can recognize by the tone, even if they cannot hear the words, an adult's mood or response to something they are doing. But listening to the sound of words can be introduced quite early as part of the climate of literacy, through songs, rhymes and games. The children may not consciously realize that words which end with the same sound are said to rhyme, but it is only on the basis of many experiences of enjoying nursery rhymes and songs and verses and poetry that they will later be able to understand what a rhyme is and to hear and distinguish similar word endings. Children do, after all, play with sounds in babbling before they learn to speak, and they may be interested in strange names and 'funny' words by the time they are in the infant school. The teacher's responsibility here is to give them opportunities for listening, and to encourage them to notice.

A very simple example of printed material which encourages children to notice the relationship between letters and sounds is referred to in *i.t.a. An Independent Evaluation.** As happens in many schools in the reception class, the children's pegs were marked by a symbol (eg a rose or a ship). For her own convenience, the teacher had made a chart of the children's names in i.t.a. and the corresponding symbols. The children had their names written (again in i.t.a.) on cards to hang round their necks. The account continues '... the reception class teacher was amazed when, within their first few days at school, the children began to look at the list in the cloak-

* F W Warburton and V Southgate

room and remark on similar letters which appeared in each other's names'. There had at this stage been no teaching of phoneme/grapheme relationships. Although this occurred during an experiment with i.t.a., it is a good example of the kind of material which is a useful background to reading taught by any method, using the medium of t.o. as well as that of i.t.a. The children know their own names and soon learn those of the rest of the class. They are interested in names: their own name is a very important part of them (which is why it is so easy to hurt a child by teasing him about his name). They are likely, therefore, to examine such a list and notice things about it: another child's name which begins with the same letter as their own, for example.

Another useful chart may be made of a rhyme or poem which the children enjoy, and come to know by heart through listening to it, perhaps acting it or joining in when the teacher reads it. Here words which end in the same sound may well have similar letter-endings, and this is useful background experience which may or may not be consciously noticed by the children initially. Later, when they are aware that there is a relationship between letters and combinations of letters and sounds, they can learn still more from rhymes. Songs the children sing can also usefully be printed as a chart. Again, they learn the words through singing the songs, and so in a sense they can 'read' the printed song. If the teacher sometimes run her hand along under the words as they sing them, the left to right movement in reading is again demonstrated, and the chart may help them to acquire a sight vocabulary, as well as to begin to notice similarities between words.

b SYSTEMATIC TEACHING

The timing and extent of the introduction of systematic teaching of phonics is a matter for the individual teacher to decide, but her decision may be guided by the children's progress.

If the children's first primers and reading material are to call forth a thoughtful and imaginative response, then they have to use at least some words which cannot be worked out through a knowledge of simple, basic phonics.

Furthermore, there is a good deal of evidence that one of the children's greatest difficulties in using their knowledge of phonics in reading is that of blending discrete sounds into a word: there is, in fact, a great deal to be said, simply in order to teach phonics more effectively, for avoiding this problem by learning the sounds of the letters *within words* rather than learning letter sounds, and then trying consciously to combine them. Hunter Diack makes the point very clearly: 'The sounds that the letters *c-a-t* stand for in *cat* are not *ker-a-ter* but the sounds in the word cat. To ask a child at this early age to put together *ker-a-ter* and make "cat" is asking him to do the impossible. The idea is too abstract for the very young child.'*

So there is a strong case to be made for introducing phonics as a decoding skill at a point when the children are already reading their first primers, and coming up against new words whose meaning they cannot unlock through illustrations or obvious contextual clues, so that the purpose is clear and the situation in which the new skill can be used is already there, and (if the material is interesting and relevant, as it should be) the need is pressing. At the same time the basic sight vocabulary which is built up provides the teacher with material (ie known words) from which she can teach in the most effective way.

The teacher may approach this from either of two rather different viewpoints: she may teach phonics as and when the need arises in the course of the children's reading, or she may make a list of the most common phonograms the children are likely to meet and devise teaching situations for teaching these on a regular basis; or, of course, she may do both.

In fact it is helpful for a teacher (and especially for an inexperienced one) to make such a list whether she expects to teach phonics only incidentally and informally, or more regularly and systematically, for two reasons: because it will help her to gain a detailed knowledge of the books and reading materials the children are to use so that she becomes aware of many opportunities for teaching and learning, and because it can provide an overall picture of work to be done and a record of what has been accomplished. Some books provide lists of sounds to be taught, but the most useful and effective list is often one which the teacher makes for herself. The list need not be complete to begin with. It is perhaps better if it grows as time goes on, because this means that the teacher is flexible in following through her plans and learning from the children's needs and the changing situation to make helpful modifications. But a preliminary list, based on a careful

* *In Spite of the Alphabet*

examination of the reading materials, is a good beginning, because it helps a teacher to plan ahead.

A useful list will probably include the following:

(i) Initial letter sounds are very helpful in guessing what a word, met in context, must be, so the list will probably begin with these—not necessarily in alphabetical order at this stage, but in the order in which the children have met and will meet them.

(ii) Short vowels—a e i o u (again, probably not in alphabetical order, but in the order in which they will be met, based on words the children already know).

(iii) Long vowels including the rule about the silent *e* at the end of a word, as in *make*. The ones most frequently used in many early reading books include ay ee oo ie ou ow ea, but only a careful examination of the reading scheme to be used can establish the order for teaching purposes.

(iv) Consonant blends, for example bl, pl, ch, sh, th, wh, gr, sp, st, etc.

(v) Common word endings, eg ing, ly, ed, en, ck, ful, igh, ight, dge.

The list can be flexible both in use and in composition, being added to as the teacher examines the reading material in the class and as the need arises among the children. It is often helpful if the sounds within the groups in the list are arranged in the sequence in which the teacher expects the children to meet them in their reading. But rigidity is a mistaken policy. Even if the teacher goes carefully through the reading scheme and orders her list of sounds accordingly, the background to reading, the climate of literacy which is such a vital and important part of the whole, means that all the words which the children read and write in the course of an active, interesting, thoughtful school day cannot be foreseen and may not fit into the sequence laid down, so that an excellent opportunity for teaching a particular phonogram may occur relatively unexpectedly. A list made in this way one year may prove a good starting point for next year's list. The teacher's own list (rather than one taken unaltered from a book) makes for teaching closely adapted to individual needs and to the particular books being used.

Such a list should not make for rigidity in teaching methods. It can be particularly useful to a teacher who expects to teach phonics largely incidentally and informally, because it provides her with an overall picture of work to be done, a record of what has been accomplished and what she hopes to achieve for each child, and brings a sense of order to her planning. Every child may be in a different position as regards his knowledge of phonics, but she knows where each child is.

It also makes it possible to use games and other devices in teaching, because the teacher sees where they fit into the overall plan, and where the gaps, if any, occur. If a teacher has decided to use a set of published phonic materials, the list will be helpful, by showing her how to relate these to the books the children are reading, or going to read, and where they may most effectively be introduced.

Of course the list should not become a Procrustean bed into which every child has to fit. Phonics is not an end in itself; some children find it immensely helpful as a means of tackling new words, but there are some who learn to read without apparently learning phonics at all, at any rate consciously, and who may even find it a stumbling block. Professor Burt* points out that there are differences in children's imagery and states that 'The effective use of phonic methods is scarcely possible without good auditory imagery. And the dull, for the most part, are predominantly visualisers'. So that a teacher should try to vary her teaching according to the needs and abilities of the children in this, as in everything else. But for many children an understanding of the alphabetical principle is enlightening.

The teaching need not be dull. It should not be a series of drills. To begin with, every sound and possible phonogram does not have to be taught, if the chidren learn how to learn intelligently and actively. As they grow older and more experienced, having understood the alphabetic principle and how to use their knowledge, they can often apply the principles to new word sounds.

Secondly, the actual learning and the necessary practice can be enjoyable. Carefully planned games can be an effective way of both teaching and practising phonics. They have many advantages: they provide opportunities for new learning as well as for practice, and for children to work and learn together. When the teacher is playing with the children, they

* Preface by Sir Cyril Burt to *i.t.a. An Independent Evaluation*

often provide her with a useful opportunity for noticing individual children's strengths and weaknesses, and for deciding when a child seems ready for a new step in learning.

Games

One of the most useful games to begin with is 'I Spy'. If this is played with a group of children, the teacher can draw attention to the letter/sound relationship by printing each word as it is guessed on the blackboard or a poster for all the children to see, putting words beginning with the same sound directly under each other.

The game can be considerably developed: it need not be confined to single initial letters, but digraphs (ch, st, bl for example) can be used, and the number of possible objects can be increased by using pictures, either big posters of scenes, or a number of discrete objects cut out of magazines and mounted on large sheets. (This can usefully be done by the children themselves when they are old enough, for use in games either for themselves or for younger children.) The game can later be played with word endings, as well as with word beginnings, but it is important to direct attention to the beginning of a word until left-right movements in reading are thoroughly established.

As soon as the children begin to know the initial letter sounds, these should be used as an additional clue to a new word. In reading a sentence printed under a picture, a knowledge of the sound of even the first letter of the unknown word is a great help towards deciphering it, especially in conjunction with the visual clues provided by the illustration and the contextual clues provided by the sentence.

For practice in word endings, the game of 'Threes' described on p. 108 may become a rhyming game, in which there is one word card and two picture cards depicting objects, the name of which rhyme with the word card: eg

sing

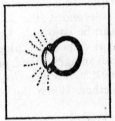

There are a number of published games which can be usefully fitted into a teacher's plan: eg *Reading Games* by Betty Root, which include *I Spy* and a whole series of other games giving practice in the recognition of phoneme/grapheme relationships which can be played by children in the infant school; and Stott's *Programmed Reading Kit*, which was originally planned for older backward children and which has been recently revised. The kit includes games through which the children learn to blend as well as to recognize letter sounds. This blending is not explicitly taught—Stott regards such explicit teaching as a cause of confusion—but allows 'the true fusion of sounds as they occur in words [to] take place below the level of consciousness, following the visual sequence of the letters'.*

Nonsense Characters and Stories

One of the drawbacks to a purely phonic approach to reading, already mentioned, is that if words in the books the children read are chosen *only* because they are at the appropriate phonic level they are likely to be dull, if not meaningless; and if all the necessary practice is included in the text of the book, its sentences are likely to include many vain repetitions. But it is possible to make up and enjoy short sentences with words which are short and regular in a light-hearted way, especially if these are sometimes embedded in stories, as with a cat who sat on the magic mat. The Dr Seuss books are good examples of how it is possible to have fun with sounds by making up nonsense stories, eg *The Cat in the Hat* and *Hop on Pop* and all the rest. Children can make up more crazy characters with names which use given sounds, and illustrate them with a lively imagination—The Pig in the Wig, or the Big Fat Man for example. In printing the name under the character, and in looking at all the pictures and names other children have made, there is much helpful practice in using phonics.

Action Words

There are action words too—*hop stop* (always a useful word to teach early on!) *sit run jump clap*—which may be printed

* The Second International Reading Symposium, edited by Downing and Brown, p 192

on cards, the appropriate action being made when the card is shown. This can be expanded to sentences using the children's names, written on the blackboard by the teacher (giving the children another opportunity of watching while a word is printed, and so another experience of the sequence of letters and sounds in time) such as *Bill, hop to Jim*; *Mary, run to Peter*; *Jane, clap ten*. Such practice becomes a game. (If this is too disruptive or there is not enough room, children can imagine that the first two fingers on their right hand are legs which run or jump or hop over a table.)

The omission of any rule concerning the age at which children should begin to learn phonics is deliberate. So much depends on the children and on the teacher: on the children's speech and language experience, their individual abilities, strengths and weaknesses, and on the teacher's own temperament and the way in which she finds she can teach most effectively. But perhaps the surest guide is the child's own progress. Phonics will be introduced at the point when it seems most useful for him as a decoding device, and when he is able to profit by it. If it is introduced gradually, then his progress is the teacher's indication. If learning to listen is part of the climate of literacy, the teaching of phonics is not, in any case, going to start for every child at a given moment. Clearly, a simple game of 'I Spy' might be played quite informally with a group of children very early in their learning to read, and the teacher can base her judgment on the readiness of individuals for the next stage by their response. Specific teaching will continue as the children meet more and more words in their reading.

Visual, kinaesthetic and phonic methods of learning to read all work together to help each other. Through teaching based initially on the words in his basic sight vocabulary, a child begins to learn the letter/sound relationships; a growing knowledge of phonics provides him with clues to new words which he meets in the course of his reading. Through use, these gradually become part of his sight vocabulary, and in its turn his sight vocabulary provides a reservoir of known words for a child to refer to, when he comes across a new word he cannot immediately recognize or decode, to see whether any of the known words have phoneme/grapheme relationships which he can use.

If specific teaching in particular skills is set against the general background in which reading is an important part of the life of the group, then the purpose of such skills is clear, and the occasions for putting them to use occur immediately.

NOTES ON BOOKS FOR FURTHER READING

There is a paper by D H Stott on *Programmed Methods in the Teaching of Reading* published in *The Second International Reading Symposium* (1967), which not only provides an introduction to the Stott *Programmed Reading Kit* but also sets out briefly but clearly reasons for teaching phonics, and suggestions as to how this may be done effectively.

There are sections on teaching phonics in *The Teaching of Reading* by Donald Moyle and in A E Tansley's *Reading and Remedial Reading*.

In Spite of the Alphabet, by Hunter Diack, argues the case for phonic methods of teaching reading.

All these books contain references and bibliographies.

5

Planning Work with a Class:
the importance of records

Records have to be kept to a minimum because of the time factor: some can be made out of school hours, but some have to be jotted down in the course of the school day, and there is little enough time with each child as it is. Out of school, teachers have their own lives to live, and if too much 'spare time' is spent on records, on preparing lessons and making teaching materials, there is too little time left to lead a normal life. But some records there must be, if sound plans for future teaching are to be made, based on a knowledge of the children and what they have done.

Such plans are specially worthwhile for an inexperienced teacher, because they give her confidence, and help her to make day-to-day decisions. They help her to feel, and indeed to be, in control of the situation, and her confidence will communicate itself to the children. Particularly in a first teaching job, everyday demands can be almost overwhelming and very tiring. To be able to stand back and look at the whole situation from time to time, when the children are not there, considering records of what has been done, can be very valuable and considerably less exhausting than trying to teach a group of children without adequate planning.

There is another important point too. Some children have difficulties in learning. Records will help the teacher to become aware of these, and the first step in solving a problem is to be aware that it exists. (It is surprising how often this awareness alone seems helpful.)

a PLANS

Making a plan of the learning activities and work to be done in the course of a period (a week, a term, a school year—the amount of detail possible in such a plan will vary according to the length of the period) does not mean that the teaching must be formal, or rigid, or that the plan will be inflexibly followed. On the contrary, the freer the children are to be, the more necessary it is for the teacher to plan carefully. To give a simple example, if the children are going to get out and put away books and materials and apparatus for themselves, then such things must be carefully organized on the shelves, perhaps colour-coded, and simple procedures for getting and replacing things have to be arranged with the children, taught and followed.

If there is to be systematic teaching of reading, then there must be a carefully worked-out overall plan. It can be thought of as though it were a map for a journey. It provides a view of the whole countryside to be explored, and the possible routes to be taken, with all the different features in the landscape (including some of the hazards) which may be encountered, or which should be seen, on the way. Individual records then show the different paths taken by the children through the country stretching before them. If the teacher considers these from time to time, she knows where each child is and how to help him if he is stuck, or if he is running into difficulty. The children may all be in different places, and perhaps following different routes, or most of them may be travelling at differing speeds along a main highway with perhaps a few individuals trying new tracks, but if the teacher knows the whereabouts of each child, the country through which they are all travelling, and the ultimate destination, then the children can follow many paths at their own pace, and no one will be lost. The teaching records will be related to the type of country and routes to be followed, the learning records to the whereabouts of every child.

The general map or plan for reading will contain an outline of skills to be covered in a given period—not in the expectation that every child will progress through to the hoped-for destination, but simply that the teacher may see where she is going, and how all the different learning situations she plans fit in with the whole.

(a) To begin with, there will be the pre-reading activities and experiences, opportunities for speaking and listening, for putting ideas into words, for learning what reading is, for discovering the purpose and satisfaction of books and stories.

(b) Then will come the children's first encounters with reading and printing themselves, arising from their own active learning, and a growing understanding of what words and letters are.

(c) The next stage may be planning for the shared experiences which will provide common ground and common vocabulary, for introducing a reading scheme. (Words to be used frequently in captions might be included in the teacher's notes.)

(d) Any published plan of the reading scheme or schemes to be used should be noted, with the points at which any ancilliary materials are to be introduced. (Such materials may be part of the scheme, or teacher-made, or both.) This will include apparatus for teaching phonics. It is useful to make a chart showing how all this fits together. Some reading schemes provide such a chart, which can be very helpful, and should be kept among the records. This should include a note of any points in the reading scheme where teaching to anticipate difficulties is important. An example of a bridging game, teaching children new words before they meet them in a book, is given on page 115, but a note of any specially difficult words, sentences or ideas in a new book is useful. This is the kind of information which comes with experience. A beginning teacher cannot be expected to anticipate problems, but if she keeps a note of the difficulties the children actually encounter as they arise, her plans became more and more effective in subsequent years.

(e) Plans for introducing phonics and other methods of attack on new words should be included.

(f) Activities in which the children read and use their new skills outside the reading scheme will occur all the time. A note of some possibilities may be helpful to a beginner to make sure full advantage is taken of any opportunities that arise and as a reminder of the importance of encouraging reading outside systematic teaching. An experienced teacher will do this without having to think about it consciously, but it is more difficult to remember when one is fully responsible for a class for the first time.

(g) Plans for teaching further reading skills should be included. There is such a wide variation in children's backgrounds, abilities and interests that even if no child in the class can read at the beginning of the year, some may be reading surprisingly well by the end of it.

If the teacher does not plan to use any published reading scheme, but to make her own, then a fairly complete plan of the kinds of materials she expects to use (including books made by the teacher and the children and any printed books which may be incorporated) gives an overall view of what will be needed. This can then be checked against what is already available in the classroom. A list of vocabulary used in early reading material is important.

b RECORDS

General records

As well as a plan of what she hopes to do, the teacher needs a record of what has actually been done.

This might include the following:

Words

A list of words used frequently in the classroom, which the children may be expected to recognize by sight, is very helpful. (Individual lists may be kept for some children—perhaps for all who are just beginning to learn to read, especially if the teacher is not using any published reading scheme.)

When a reading scheme is introduced, a list of the words in the first books is useful, especially if a basic sight vocabulary is going to be built up as a source of known words for teaching phonics and other reading skills. An example of this kind of simple record is shown on page 74. The list itself is *not* a test to be shown to the children, but the teacher might print each word on a separate card, and go through them with each child individually to see how many he can recognize, checking the list herself privately afterwards, but encouraging the child, no matter how few words he knows.

The following points about this example may be helpful:

(a) The record is for the first *three* pre-readers*—not for the

* of *One, Two, Three and Away!*

first book alone. This is because a child who can read the first pre-reader, when the words are met in context and when he has illustrations to help him, cannot be expected to recognize them when they are met individually out of context, and if he is, his pleasure and confidence in reading may be diminished. Furthermore, he will meet the same words (and particularly the words other than nouns, which cannot be illustrated and are often better learned in context) again and again in the first books, and there is not much point in checking whether he knows them individually until he has had a chance to learn them. They are, too, words which he is likely to meet in notices and captions around the classroom, as well as in his books, and the more experience he has before being

1, 2, 3 and Away! Introductory Books A, B & C

		Peter	John	Mary	David	Ann	Melanie	Pat	Kevin
A	Roger	✓	✓	✓	✓	✓	✓	✓	✓
	Red-hat	✓	✓	✓	✓		✓		✓
	here			✓			✓		
	is	✓	✓	✓		✓	✓		✓
	hat	✓	✓	✓	✓	✓	✓		✓
	red	✓	✓	✓	✓	✓	✓	✓	✓
	Rip	✓	✓	✓			✓		✓
	dog	✓	✓	✓	✓	✓	✓		
	Mr.			✓			✓		
	Mrs.			✓			✓		
	the	✓	✓	✓		✓			✓
	house	✓	✓	✓	✓	✓	✓		
	white		✓	✓		✓	✓		
	has		✓	✓			✓		✓
	roof	✓	✓	✓		✓	✓		✓
	and		✓	✓			✓		
	door	✓	✓	✓		✓	✓		✓
	lives						✓		
	in	✓	✓				✓		✓
	the	✓	✓	✓			✓		✓
	with						✓		
	Village with three corners	✓	✓	✓	✓	✓	✓		✓
B	Billy	✓	✓		✓	✓	✓	✓	✓
	Blue-hat	✓	✓	✓	✓	✓	✓		✓
	blue		✓	✓		✓	✓		✓
	live						✓		
C	Johnny	✓	✓	✓	✓	✓	✓		✓
	Jennifer	✓	✓	✓	✓	✓	✓		✓
	Yellow-hat	✓	✓	✓	✓	✓	✓		✓
	Grandmother			✓			✓		
	Grandfather	✓	✓	✓			✓		✓
	yellow		✓	✓		✓	✓		✓

asked to recognize them out of context the better.

(b) Records are made to be used. Looking at this record, the teacher will note that Mary, Melanie, Kevin and John are ready for the next book. (The teacher may have underestimated Melanie's reading ability; her attention is then directed to the child, to watch what she is reading by choice, and whether she is being given enough to stimulate her interest and use her ability to the full.) Pat has probably been introduced to the books too quickly; the teacher is alerted to look at his individual record and consider what should be done to help him. David recognizes the names of the characters, but few other words. He probably needs more experience outside the books before continuing to read them. Most of the children except Mary and Melanie seem to be having difficulty with certain words, ie *here, live(s), with,* and confusing others, ie *Mr* and *Mrs, Grandmother* and *Grandfather.*

The teacher can plan to take the children as a group, and direct their attention to these words and the differences between them, using the words in a context outside the primers first, and returning to the books later.

Phonograms

A list of phonograms as described in the last chapter should be included. If the list has a horizontal axis showing the children's names, a brief record of phonograms recognized by each child is then available. Again, the teacher will not expect every child to learn every sound in order as presented. But her record will show the sounds she has covered in her teaching, and the children's response. This list, too, is not a check list to be presented to the children: they may recognize a sound as part of a word, when they cannot recognize it as a phonogram. It is part of the *teacher's* records.

Notes of stories and poems read, with dates

Beginning teachers may find it useful to add a very brief note on how these were received and any special activities which developed as part of them. Some of the stories and poems will be part of the overall plan; some may be introduced because a perfect opportunity arises in the course of the day.

Books

It is helpful to have a record of all the published reading material used by the children, including the books in the reading scheme or schemes and supplementary reading material.

If this seems too much, then at least a list of the sequence of readers, which may be checked against the names of the children as each child finishes a book, and the dates of finishing, should be made. Such a list can be kept up to date by the children themselves. A difficulty with this arrangement may be that it invites comparisons between those who have read many books and those who have read none. Human beings unfortunately tend to build up their own egos by disparaging others less able than themselves and comparisons will occur often enough anyway without encouragement. So any record kept by a child is best if it is his own personal record in a book, rather than a general sheet on the wall to be used by all children.

Individual Records

Some teachers keep a file for every child. This has advantages in that any notes, records of tests, samples of work, and so on can be added to the file, but the place for this is the filing cabinet in the office. The teacher still needs a brief individual record of what she learns about the children in the course of the day.

The simplest way of keeping this is to have a loose-leaf note book (carefully kept where only the teacher will see it) in which a page (or more) is devoted to each child, with his name and age at the top, and where the teacher notes at the end of the day anything which may be important for his learning which has occurred.

There should be notes on all children in the course of a term; notes on their physical development, especially if there is any problem connected with sight, hearing, or muscular co-ordination, and on their physical well-being, including notes of frequent short absences or longer periods away from school.

If a child seems tired and listless, this too may be noted: it may be that he is not getting enough sleep (in some experiments in America, progress in reading was increased by giving such children an opportunity to rest in school) or it may be that he is not well, or under some strain.

There should be notes of the children's special strengths and weaknesses, or ways in which they seem to be learning most effectively; notes on special interests, or opportunities which they have for learning or for contributing to the class as a whole (eg the fact that a parent was a bus driver or an ornithologist might come under this heading). The notes will rightly lengthen on those who seem to have special difficulties, because the teacher will be using all her knowledge in trying to think of ways in which to help them, and most people cannot remember all the little pieces of information they learn about a child which might be useful: eg a record of a special interest in motor cars might prove useful in helping a child who seemed uninterested in reading to make his first own book.

Of course, not everything will be recorded, if only because there isn't time; but as she becomes more experienced a teacher learns to note and select information likely to be of use, and the very fact that she is keeping such records may help her to note and remember little things which come up in the course of the day.

Not all teachers use note books, though it is helpful if at least summaries of information can all be in the same place. Some teachers keep a card in each child's primer, as soon as the child begins work on a reading scheme, and make a note on it each time they hear the child read: a note of the date and page, and also of any difficulties, words not known, phonograms taught, etc, so that next time the child comes to them with the book, they are reminded of anything needing special help and teaching. Such notes on cards can be summarized briefly in the main record book from time to time.

If children are taken in groups in order to teach a special reading skill, then a group record, with notes on individual variations and difficulties, may be useful. But groups change and children are absent, so individual records are important too.

From time to time, the teacher then goes through her notes, looking for points which will help her to plan for each child's learning. For some children, she may find that she has made many entries; for some only a few; perhaps for some children none at all, other than a note of the book they have just finished. This in itself may be revealing: some of these children may be doing very well; but some may be withdrawn children, who have a pressing need for the teacher's attention but who never demand it, and she is then alerted to the fact that they are being overlooked. (It is easy for any teacher, and especially a beginner, to give more time to children who insistently claim her attention.)

If a teacher herself is ill, or moves to another school, records can be invaluable to her substitute. A brief summary of important points made at the end of the year, and passed on to the new teacher or the new school, can again be immensely useful in assisting the next teacher to plan her work and in alerting her to the most effective way in which she can help individual children to learn.

There are some things which a teacher knows about a child which are better left unrecorded: confidential details she may have learned from or about parents, for example. Sometimes these may be of great importance in helping the child, in which case discussion with the next teacher may be better than written record. Moral judgments are rarely helpful. The criteria should be that a record should be made when it will help the teacher to help the child. The summary of important points should be made for the child's next teacher with this in mind.

Minute by minute records of individual children

There is another kind of record which can be illuminating: an exact minute by minute record of the activities of one particular child.

This is made on a sheet of paper with a left-hand column recording the time in minutes and seconds, and the rest of the sheet made up of brief notes of exactly what the child was doing: reading his book, looking out of the window, walking over to look at something, talking to a friend, gazing into space and so on. Such a record might sometimes be made by the teacher watching the reactions of one child to a student's period of teaching, or the teacher might ask a student to make the record during one of the periods when the student is 'observing' in the classroom. When the recorded period is over, a summary can be made of how much time was spent in various learning situations, what breaks of attention occurred, how a child dealt with requests from the teacher, and made contacts with other children. The record often brings out very clearly the point that when something has been taught it has not necessarily been learned, and it can help to show the kinds of teaching and activities which compel attention and encourage the most active learning. It can show, too, how attention may be switched off, or diverted, by children who are having learning difficulties, or who are un-interested in what is being taught.

The record is only a basis for discussion. It may be used to illuminate a child's response to different methods and ways of teaching. It may throw light on the special needs or learning habits of a particular child and so help the teacher in planning future work with him.

It should perhaps be added that it takes a certain amount of courage to arrange for such a record to be made of one's own teaching. In handling and being aware of a whole group of children, the teacher's attention is so engaged, and it is so easy for her to be concerned with the teaching and organization, that a record of an individual child's response, or lack of response, can come as something of a shock. But if it makes for more effective education, the shock can only be salutary.

c INDIVIDUAL AND GROUP TEACHING

Records are useful in planning the teaching of individual children, and in indicating when a number of children may be taken together as a group because they are all at roughly the same stage or because they all need to be taught, shown or given practice in some particular skill.

It is important that the teacher should hear each child read as often as she can. When she is working with one child, she has a special opportunity to encourage him, to discover and note any difficulties he has, and help him to overcome them.

She notes not only his errors, but the *kind* of errors he makes: whether he reads steadily from left to right in both sentences and words, or needs help with this; whether he looks at the beginning of a word first; if letters are reversed (for example d for b); if words are omitted and which words are lost in this way; how he attacks a new word; whether he remembers new words easily, or needs special help (eg, in writing or tracing them); which methods of learning seem most effective. The teacher makes a note of any new words or phonograms she teaches him during this period. She can make sure, too, that he understands what he is reading and checks the meaning of words against any illustrations, and that he uses contextual clues.

In a sense, all teaching of reading is on an individual basis, but it is rarely possible for a teacher in an ordinary class always to take each child separately. There is simply not enough time. It is in the beginning stages of learning to read that the child needs the teacher's regular help most. In a class where only two or three children are at this stage, individual help may be possible; it may also be necessary if there are one or two children who are having special difficulties in learning which a brief period with the teacher every day would help to overcome. But in most infant schools there are a large number of children at just the point in their learning when they most need the teacher. If, for example, she has a class of thirty children, to give each of them five minutes individual attention for reading every day would take $2\frac{1}{2}$ hours. Taking children in groups, at least from time to time, is inevitable.

But there is positive value in a group, too. In creating a climate of literacy, children are working together; in preparing for the introduction of a reading scheme, and in recounting background stories and discussing characters and illustrations, in learning to think about what they are reading and to make an imaginative response to the text, children help each other. As D H Stott points out, one of the things which makes older children dislike school is the learning in isolation which is sometimes imposed on them, and although infant school children are still at an age when they may relate more easily to an adult than to their peers, learning to learn together and help each other is something most teachers want to encourage.

Grouping need not be rigid, if the teacher keeps individual records and gives some thought to the arrangement of groups. She knows where each child is individually and she can draw together the children who are ready for a specific piece of teaching. Depending on the general organization in the school, this may sometimes occur spontaneously, or it may be planned by the teacher. For example, if some of the children were painting pictures of the Story People from *One, Two, Three and Away!* and were printing the names of the characters as captions for their pictures, the proper way to write Mr and Mrs, or the fact that proper names begin with capital letters, might be information needed by the whole group. If a number of children were setting up a post office, the need to learn how to address letters might emerge from the activity. But to utilize and devise situations in which reading and writing are *wholly* taught in this way is very difficult, especially if reading is to be taught systematically. It is usually more effective to

Plate 5

Photograph/Lois Myers

*A child discovers that Mrs. Blue-hat, with whom
she has been playing, is to be found in a book. Later, she will read
stories about her and about the other Story People.*

Plate 6

Photograph/Patrick McCullagh

*A model of a 'new world' made by a group of
secondary school children of mixed ability, while they were
reading* Adventures in Space *and other stories.*

plan systematic teaching and take children who are ready to learn or practise a particular skill in a group together. The teaching need not necessarily be formal: it might take the form of a game; but a brief period of straight-forward teaching, helping children to understand and develop a new skill, has its place too.

The number of groups in a classroom will vary, depending partly on the children and partly on the skill of the teacher. The rest of the class must be using the time profitably, but reasonably quietly, while the teacher's attention is given to the group. The whole class need not be all doing the same thing at once. Some might be painting, making models, reading in the library corner, playing a quiet game, writing, arranging pictures and captions to make a book, measuring, recording, or any other quiet activities. If the teacher's attention is to be given to a group, it is important that these activities are ones which the children can carry out without constant reference to her. This might be a time when a child is copying out a notice he has written, which is going to be pinned up on the board, or a poem to go in his own anthology. For children who can read and who enjoy reading it is a time when they can read books of their own choice for their own pleasure. The skill of teaching the particular group, but at the same time keeping an eye over the rest of the class, is one which comes with experience, and in any case it is usually best to plan for a break between groups, in which the teacher can go round and give brief encouragement to those who are working at other things.

One of the drawbacks to dividing children into semi-permanent groups is that, whereas it may be an incentive to work if a child is in the top group, or even in one of the middle groups, it can be very discouraging always to be in the bottom group: children establish their idea of themselves chiefly through the reactions of other people to them, measuring themselves also against their peers. If they find themselves unable to do something most of the others can do, they may begin to regard themselves as failures and even to accept their lack of progress. We should avoid labelling them at any age. Unfortunately, the groups may be called red, green, blue and yellow, or sputniks, butterflies, aeroplanes and robins, but in any rigid grouping the children soon begin to refer to 'the top group', 'the bottom group', 'the middle group', etc. The answer to this problem lies only partly in the teacher's own attitude and terminology.

Flexibility of grouping is a greater help. Inevitably, the same children come together on many occasions, but for some games, for example, good and poor readers may be grouped together. Flexible grouping simply means that the teacher calls together into a group children who are at a stage to profit by a particular piece of teaching: it might be to learn a new phonogram (presented through words they already know) or to read some sentences, or to discuss a story they have heard. In the first two groupings, the children are probably those at roughly the same reading level, but not necessarily in the last grouping: the teacher might have chosen to read a story from one of the primers to the group, and some of the children could be those meeting the story for the first time, while others have already read it for themselves. A group of children of varying achievement and ability may come together to read a story dramatically, different children reading different parts, some of which are much easier than others. Again, careful planning by the teacher is needed so that each child is given a part within his capabilities. In playing a reading game, it is often really helpful to include a child who is good at reading with others who are not as advanced, so that he may help them, and the idea of those who can do something well helping others who find it difficult is one to which children will respond.

In a school where there is vertical grouping, an older child sometimes helps a younger one. The National Association of Head Teachers also suggested that senior pupils in secondary schools should be allowed time in school hours to read and talk to young children in nursery and infant schools as part of their own education.*

The size of the group will vary, too, according to the age and ability of the children, and the particular purpose for which it has been formed: it might be two or three one day and ten the next. The most useful average size is probably about six for discussion and for the most effective use of teacher time, but obviously there may be times when the teacher will take two children, and times when she may have the whole class together for a story, or a discussion of something which affects everyone. But the simple fact which has been learned over the years is that children can be taught to read

* This suggestion was made in written evidence to the Bullock committee of inquiry into reading standards, as reported in *The Times*, 6 November 1972.

more effectively if they are not taught all the time as a whole class.

Records help the teacher to plan ahead, so that when she goes into the classroom in the morning she has planned which children she expects to take in which group, what the many will be doing while she is teaching the few, and how materials will be organized so that the children can work independently. The plan need not be rigidly adhered to. The more experienced she is, the more flexibility the teacher will be able to achieve. But a plan is a great confidence-builder for the inexperienced, and thinking out the sheer practical details of organization and materials alone in advance can free the beginning teacher from many avoidable problems.

NOTES ON BOOKS FOR FURTHER READING

Every teacher has to make her own plan and to decide the kind of records most suitable for her work with the children, but the following sections of books mentioned elsewhere in this text are relevant.

In *The Teaching of Reading* there is a chapter on *Matters of Organization*, in which Donald Moyle includes two samples of brief individual records, and discusses group and individual work. There is also a useful chapter on *The Keeping of Records* in *Teaching the Slow Learner in the Primary School*, ed. by M F Cleugh. The chapter on *Failure in Reading*, in *Basic Teaching for Slow Learners* by Peter Bell, contains a list of steps in phonic instruction which might be useful in making an overall plan, but which is not intended to be followed rigidly by the children.

PART THREE

Late Starters

6

Teaching the beginnings of reading in Junior, Middle and Secondary Schools

A chapter on teaching older children to read might seem out of place in a book 'for anyone teaching the early stages of reading ... for the first time'. Remedial education demands a high degree of skill from a knowledgeable and experienced teacher. However, it is nonetheless true that a number of young teachers, and teachers whose previous experience has not included the teaching of reading, suddenly find themselves responsible for older children who cannot read.

The causes of backwardness* in general, and of failure in reading in particular, are many. 'Reading' itself is not one skill, but a complex of related skills, and the results of a great deal of research have been published since the war which are relevant to the teaching of reading. Furthermore, every child responds to learning situations in his own individual way, bringing to it his own background of experience and attitudes. He needs to be studied as an individual, especially when he is experiencing difficulties in learning, and the data which can be collected about him must be interpreted. Nonetheless, there are some general principles which a beginning teacher can follow, while she is learning more about the children, and more about the teaching of reading. She has to meet her class tomorrow morning, and to plan her work in order to give all the children in her care, whatever their problems and abilities, as many opportunities for growth, for learning and for satisfactory development as she can.

a   CAUSES OF FAILURE IN LEARNING TO READ

Reading is a complex skill and the causes of failure in learning

* 'Backward' is used here in the sense of falling behind contemporaries in school work, for whatever cause. It is not meant to imply mental retardation.

to read are rarely simple. The main cause may lie in the child's home and background, in the child himself, or in the school. But wherever the principal reason is found, it is rarely found alone.

Causes in the home environment

The roots of the problem may lie in the child's general background. Obviously, a home in which a child is physically well-cared for, in which he has enough rest and suitable food, in which he is loved and given a place but also taught and controlled, a literate home in which he is talked to and read to, gives him many advantages over a child who comes from a home which lacks any or all of these things. There may be factors which cannot be changed, eg parents who speak another language or who come from another culture naturally share this with their children. It may in the end, if he can absorb this and the language he finds at school, give a child a richer background in some ways than one who is without it, but certainly when he first goes to school it can make for difficulties in language and in learning to read.

There may be emotional stresses and strains within a home, which cause a child to feel anxious. The tension may be such that it absorbs his energies and thoughts for the time being, leaving him with little strength to learn new skills. Sometimes such tensions occur in a home which is otherwise helpful, when parents are over-anxious or demand too much of a child. I taught a boy whose parents were so anxious that he should measure up to their intellectual standards that they could not allow him to have the normal interests of childhood. When he read a book, at the age of seven or eight, it had to be something at least at the reading level of a junior encyclopaedia; when they took him on holiday, they took him to the houses of parliament to hear a debate. The trouble was that he was always trying to read something too difficult for him to manage, and he felt guilty if he showed an interest in the normal activities of a boy of his age. He was an intelligent boy, but he had a reading problem because the decoding of the texts he was expected to use at home demanded so much concentration that he found it impossible to absorb much of the content.

Even a normal child in a normally happy home may have periods of exceptional emotional stress when his school work seems to suffer. The most obvious example is when another child is born, and this seems to be most important if the birth of a second child coincides with the elder child going to school: the baby inevitably absorbs the parents' attention, and when he goes to school he leaves the baby in possession. The strain comes just at the point when he is beginning to learn to read. But there are many occasions when stress can occur: the illness of parents or children, financial insecurity of which children are aware, or other anxieties and difficulties at home quite unconnected with school.

There may be nothing very much that a teacher can do about the environment in which a child moves outside school, though any serious problem endangering the child's welfare should of course be reported to the appropriate authority. The main purpose of noting the general background is to try to change what happens inside school to compensate as far as possible for any difficulties or deficiencies outside.

If a child comes from a culturally deprived background, that is all the more reason for giving him opportunities for play and the essential experiences on which language development is based. In such circumstances, it would be only reasonable to expect him to begin to learn to read rather later than more fortunate children, because he must first go through the earlier stages of learning.

If a child comes from a different cultural background, then this must be respected, and any special contribution he has to make should be sought out and accepted by the teacher. Such a child, or a group of children, provide an opportunity for teaching *all* the children in the class or school to respect other people and their way of life. A very readable and entertaining, but also perceptive and enlightening account of teaching immigrant children will be found in Rachel Scott's *A Wedding Man is Nicer than Cats, Miss.*

Causes in the child himself

The most obvious causes may be defects of sight or hearing, or that the child is developing more slowly than other children of his age and so takes longer to reach the stage when he is able to learn to read. Any illness may lower his vitality. Poor muscular co-ordination may cause difficulties.

The teacher, and particularly the beginning teacher, cannot diagnose the cause of difficulties herself. Her responsibility is to be aware of the possibility of problems of physical or mental development, to be on the watch for any signs of these, and to recommend the child for diagnosis and special help. Teachers are the only trained people in the land with whom all children frequently come into contact. Just as one of the functions of a general practitioner is to screen his patients and pass on those who need specialist treatment to the appropriate consultant, so a similar screening function is part of a teacher's responsibility. She is in a particularly strong position to do this because she sees each child within a group of children of similar age, and so she is able to make comparisons. Experience, as well as training, teaches her what behaviour and abilities to expect from children of different ages. Where any child differs greatly from his fellows, she should be on the alert.

Physical defects may be only slight—gross defects are recognized early—but they may nevertheless be an important cause of a child's initial failure. Frequent short absences for minor ailments may be a more important reason for a child falling behind in learning than a prolonged illness, because his need for special teaching to catch up is overlooked, whereas if he has been away for a term everyone sees clearly that he must be given extra help. Records are an immense help in pinpointing problems.

There may also be the possibility of specific developmental dyslexia, ie a marked disability in reading which cannot be accounted for by environmental, intellectual or emotional conditions. The existence of such a condition is still a matter of controversy and certainly the diagnosis lies outside the school. The teacher's responsibility is again to recommend that a child who continues to fail, for no apparent reason, be seen by a specialist. An interesting discussion of dyslexia, and references to modern findings, will be found in *Reading and its Difficulties* by Professor M D Vernon.

Causes within the school

Teachers are fallible human beings: mistakes are part of learning, including learning how to teach. Most experienced teachers can look back over their teaching lives and remember certain children from whom, for one reason or another, they learned a great deal about teaching. Even though we may work conscientiously and give of our best at all times (and that is a difficult enough standard to achieve), we can still make mistakes, both in our methods of teaching and in the way we handle particular children.

The important point is that we should be willing to recognize mistakes and to learn from them. A child's failure in learning to read may sometimes be caused partly by school conditions and these include not only over-large classes, but also ineffective teaching. But this does not mean that we should try to apportion blame to others. If a teacher in a junior or middle school finds that a child in her class cannot read, she has no means of immediately knowing the cause of this. She may think that the child would be reading if his earlier teaching had been different, if particular methods had been used, or if he had been handled in a different way. She may be right or she may be wrong. Even if he responds to a new method under her care—if, for example, he quickly comes to understand the alphabetic principle, and to use phonics, and this causes him to forge ahead—she still has no means of knowing whether his progress is due to maturation and the fact that she is now reaping the reward of all the background experience and teaching that has gone before, or whether he might have responded to such teaching at an earlier age. The consideration of the possibility of teacher-error is valuable chiefly when it is done by the teacher who is responsible for the child, with a view to examining her *own* teaching in order to change it if necessary.

It is part of our responsibility as teachers to continue to learn as much about teaching as we can. (The number of teachers giving up their evenings and holidays to attend courses is sufficient proof of how conscientious most teachers are in this respect.) This does not mean, of course, that one should try to follow every new idea which comes out. It does mean that new ideas should be carefully considered. No young teacher should mind asking colleagues or advisers for help with problems. And all teachers can learn something about individual children by listening to parents. A child's parents, after all, see him during most of his waking hours. They know his background as no one else can. The teacher's great advantage is that she can set what they have to say in perspective, both through her special knowledge and experience in being with many children of the same age, and because she is not as emotionally involved with the child.

One cause of backwardness in reading, or at least of failure to achieve a child's full potential, may be that the expectations which other people have of him are not too high, but too low. The teacher's organization of the class is important here. If the children are divided into groups for reading and these divisions are inflexible, a child may well come to regard himself as a non-reader and behave accordingly. Children may sometimes have to be grouped when they are learning reading skills, but the composition of the groups should be varied and the teacher's attitude must always be that the child is able to learn. He will be aware of her attitude, whether she conveys it to him consciously or not.

Another matter to be considered is the school environment and especially the classroom for which one is responsible. Is it an interesting place, with materials available which stimulate children to read and provide them with opportunities of practising the skill? This is a matter of providing wall charts and displays and making books at their level of competence freely available to the children. Lack of funds may make it difficult to provide all one could wish, but simple materials can be very effective, and pictures and displays made by the children are often more effective than those made by the teacher. The teacher's responsibility is to see that the classroom itself is part of the apparatus of learning.

b PRELIMINARY CONSIDERATIONS IN TEACHING LATE STARTERS

There are likely to be a number of children who enter the junior or middle school with minimal reading skills—some of them unable to read at all. In the ILEA Literacy Survey (1969),† 17% of eight years olds had reading scores two years behind their chronological age: in other words, they needed to begin at the very beginning. At least as many more children will need careful teaching in basic skills.†† The numbers should be smaller in the middle school, and there may be only a handful of such children by the time the secondary stage is reached; but any teacher in a junior or middle school should be prepared to teach some children the very beginnings of reading, and there should be at least one teacher in a secondary school who is able to undertake this responsibility.

This should not surprise us: in many countries children only enter school at seven, and there is some evidence that at

† This was an interim report on its 1967 Literacy Survey of 31,308 eight year old children in London.
†† The National Child Development Survey found that 44% of the 11,000 seven year old children studied needed the kind of help in reading normally given in an infant school.

this age children are likely to learn the complex skills of reading more readily than younger children. There is in any case such variation in children, in their homes and families and schools, that wide differences in the age at which they learn to read are to be expected. The real cause for surprise is that the position has not been generally recognized until recently outside the schools themselves.

If there are children with special disabilities who need special help, our responsibility as teachers is to identify them as quickly as possible; but there are likely to be still more children who can be taught to read by the methods already discussed in earlier chapters, adapted to the needs and interests of older children.

There is, however, one problem which the teacher of the late starters faces which does not arise with younger children. It has been said earlier that we learn the meaning of a word through experience: we learn what soft and hard mean by touching, or perhaps by banging into, objects; of colour by seeing colours. The books in the reading scheme may say 'I like the dog', or 'It is fun in the water', but for the child who has been frightened by a fierce dog, or pushed in at the deep end, the words 'dog 'and 'water' have a different meaning. A child who has reached the age of eight or nine and is still unable to read, has nonetheless built up a concept of reading. The word to him may mean an impossible, unintelligible task. It may be associated with the disappointment and anxiety he senses in his parents and perhaps in his teachers. At best, it is a skill which has no part in his own interests and concerns, and which he struggles to learn because this is expected of him; at worst, he may regard it as something to be avoided at all costs, and he may defend himself against the undermining of his self-esteem by asserting himself aggressively in other ways. A 'couldn't care less' attitude is often the defence of someone who finds himself unable to do something which other people regard as important and valuable. If the skill 'doesn't matter', then the fact that he can't do it doesn't matter: to recognize that one is shut out from an important area of human experience and achievement is much less bearable.

The teacher of late starters needs first to understand the feelings and attitudes of the children, as a preliminary to changing them. They have been built up by past experience; only new and different experiences will create a new attitude, and give the word 'reading' a new meaning.

But at the same time, it is clear that an important part of the new experience must be success in learning to read, and this means the planned introduction of reading material and systematic teaching.

c RESTORING THE CHILDREN'S CONFIDENCE IN THEMSELVES

Most children realize very early the importance of being able to read. Even in an infant school run on very informal lines, with integrated classes and an integrated day, reading emerges, or should emerge, as a major skill, recognized by parents and teachers to be of vital importance. As they grow older, non-readers begin to realize that their contemporaries are succeeding and they are not. More and more of their work in school depends on being able to read. Independence in learning is bound up with reading: the child who cannot follow written instructions, or look something up in a book, is inevitably dependent on someone else. The loss of confidence in themselves and their ability to learn is often a marked characteristic of such children, and this spreads from the reading situation to other areas, perhaps to their whole life. It is of first importance to try to build up a child's confidence in himself, to restore his self-respect. This means achievement, success and recognition may have to come first in some activity other than reading.

It is well worthwhile for the teacher, simply from the point of view of teaching a child to read, to search out any special talent he may have, and help him to make the most of it. This is part of every teacher's job with every child, but in the case of backward children (ie those who are failing in their school-work) it is perhaps even more important and certainly it is usually more difficult.

If a child has a special talent in handwork or music, art or games, the teacher must make the most of it. The child can be given every encouragement to develop his particular ability, and his achievement recognized—*recognized*, not over-praised, for children are quick to discern the difference between recognition of genuine achievement and effusive but indiscriminate exclamation.

Two simple examples illustrate this point.

David (not his real name) was eight years old, and unable to read. He came from a respectable, working-class home in an overcrowded area in the centre of a city. His three older brothers had no problems in learning, and although his parents didn't read much themselves, they were anxious about him, and he sensed their anxiety. He was a quiet little boy, who was in one sense no trouble in school, but he wept whenever he was given a book, because before he opened it he was sure he wouldn't be able to read it. His IQ, as measured by an individual test, was 68. Whether this was an indication of innate ability, or just a measure of his present abilities and achievements, compared to those of other children of his age, it was clear that he needed help and encouragement. He wasn't very successful in the rest of his school-work and he was too timid to play games well, but he had one talent: he had a good ear for music, and his parents gave him a mouth organ. He could play any simple tune by ear.

David was encouraged to play. He played to his teacher; he played to the class. The class was impressed, and it was clear that the teacher valued his playing, because she created opportunities for him to play still more. (This kind of recognition often means more than praise.) The headmaster heard about David, and David played to him. The rest of the school came to know him as 'the boy who can play the mouth organ'.

When a child has a talent of this kind, it is possible to include him in activities closely connected with reading, but where he does not himself have to read: playing music as part of a puppet play, for example, where a timid child can remain unseen behind the stage but make a contribution to the work of the group. As the child becomes more confident, a link can be made to reading through songs: he plays the tune and, as he listens to others singing, comes to know the words. If he is given a song book, he can then read the words of the song.

Of course this is only a beginning. When David became more confident in himself, he still had to meet his first book, and there had to be carefully planned, systematic teaching before he could read. But the first part of his remedial education began when his talent was recognized, so that he was able to build up an image of himself as someone who could learn, who could contribute to the work of the class, who was valued.

One typical incident in the school life of another boy provides a contrast. Peter (again not his real name) had great difficulty in reading, though he was a boy of at least average ability, and at school was interested chiefly in handwork of any kind. At the beginning of the autumn term in a new school, the class was asked to collect the leaves of eight different trees, and mount them in any way they liked. Most children made them into little booklets. Peter spent hours making them into a mobile. He outlined the leaves by putting them on different pieces of coloured cardboard, spraying them with paint, and then removing the leaf. The leaves were cut out, and hung from bars made from wire coat hangers, and the result was effective: it was an imaginative presentation, and the leaves moved and turned, as if blown in the wind. Peter took it to school. The teacher made barely a passing comment, and never bothered to hang it up. Peter had ability in working with his hands. The chance of recognizing a real achievement was lost and an opportunity to build a positive attitude towards a new school, a new teacher, and perhaps new learning situations was wasted. It was a small thing, but a child's life at school, and his attitudes towards himself and his work, are built through just such small happenings.

A younger child may be satisfied by his teacher's praise: if the teacher says his work is good, then it is good; he accepts the praise and is encouraged by it. But by the time he is seven or eight, simple praise is rarely enough, especially for a child who is uncertain of his own ability. Recognition of a special talent by being given opportunities to exercise it is even more important, and the teacher's judgment is no longer enough: the response of other children matters as well. As he grows older, the approval of his contemporaries becomes even more vital.

Because this kind of encouragement is so important in reassuring a child that he is the kind of person who can learn and in persuading him to make the necessary effort to overcome his difficulties in the 3Rs, one should avoid taking him away from activities he enjoys and can succeed in, in order to give him extra teaching in reading. If children have to be withdrawn from a class, the period should be timed, if this is at all possible, when an activity which he greatly enjoys, or in which he has a chance of special success, is not going on.

Where a child has a special ability, the solution to the problem of maintaining or re-establishing his self-esteem is often relatively straightforward; the real difficulty is that there are some children who seem to have no special talents. They seem always to be outshone by other children of the same age, whatever they do. There is no easy answer to this problem, but some of the following suggestions may prove useful.

Plate 7

Photograph/Patrick McCullagh

This group and the one shown on Plate 8 are from the class which made the space model. They are writing a space adventure story. One member of the group has been appointed to do the actual writing, while the others make suggestions. Seven is about the maximum number for such a group.

Plate 8

Photograph/Patrick McCullagh

Operating a robot made by the children in connection with
their reading of space adventure stories

*Children at the secondary stage may still find the creation
of a three-dimensional imaginary world a stimulating background
for discussion and written work.*

(a) A child without special talents may nonetheless have special knowledge. His father may have racing pigeons or work on the railways, he may keep rabbits, or help in the market on Saturdays; he may come from another area, or another country, and so have something extra to contribute to a project. If he has any such special interest or information, he should be given the opportunity to share it with the class.

(b) The setting provided for a child's work often enhances it, both in his own eyes and in that of others. Mounting his picture before pinning it up on the wall is a simple example of this; a model, or a scene created by a child, set in a box, laid on one side, and lit like a miniature stage, using concealed torch bulbs and batteries, is another. A carefully chosen background of sheets of coloured paper will often set off clay or other models made by the children. The fact that the teacher bothers to do this herself, or provides the materials so that the children can arrange such settings, in itself demonstrates to the child that his work has value in her eyes, as well as giving it every chance to win more general recognition.

(c) The problem of encouraging self-esteem may be a general one in the whole group, if the classes in a school are streamed, or if the children belong to a special remedial class, or remedial group. This may be the only way to give them the remedial education they need; certainly it gives the teacher a chance to give the children special experiences and opportunities which earn status for them in the eyes of their fellows, so that, instead of being regarded as 'the D stream' they become 'that class which goes out to interesting places', or undertakes some unusual activity. Individual children can find a special place for themselves, with the recognition that comes from having a useful job to do within the group. In an unstreamed group, the less able children rarely have the chance to be 'leaders', and have less chance to take responsibility, or to shine in some achievement.

An interesting expedition, properly prepared for and carried through, is one way of building up the morale of a class. There are many others. Elizabeth Taylor's *Experiment With a Backward Class*, in which she describes how the children performed a play, and set up a postal service within the school, is still worth reading. A radio 'broadcast' with a microphone plugged into a receiver is another activity which may effectively raise the children's opinion of themselves in their own eyes and in those of other children. (Many opportunities exist for linking this kind of experience with work in the 3Rs.) Some activities depend on the teacher's own interests and abilities: I have seen sword dances performed with great pride (with wooden swords, painted silver, made by the boys) in a special school, and groups of backward children composing and recording their own tunes.

The setting of the children's work is again important and some of the modern 'hardware' can be useful here. A tape-recording of a play may be more effective than a live reading, because mistakes can be eliminated before it is played outside the group. The children can listen to it themselves, and decide what needs to be cut out and whether parts should be read again. Incidental music and sound effects add to the perform-ance; they also provide opportunities for the less generally successful children to gain recognition by playing an essential part in the work of the group. In a play about a dragon or a monster, for example, all the creature has to do is to roar; but the part is usually a coveted one, and even a child (or several children) who cannot read can take it. Such a recording might be used with a live performance of puppets, and shown to a group of younger children. A play of this kind does not take the place of spontaneous drama; it serves a different function, and younger rather than older children are often a good audience for a remedial group. The performers feel that they are more competent than the audience, and younger children are not destructively critical, nor are they patronizing.

The same advantage in being able to look critically at one's own work and eliminate mistakes before presenting it to any-one outside the group occurs when simple films are made with a backward class. I have made a number of films with groups of children between the ages of nine and twelve who were virtually non-readers. They were very simply made: I handled the 8mm camera, but the children planned the story and arranged all the scenes, actors and action. (Older children might have been cameramen as well, but with these groups it was important that the setting should support their efforts as much as possible, and in this situation even an inexperi-enced adult is able to shoot the scenes more effectively than young children: for one thing, she will see that all the actors are included.) Such films have special advantages: they provide a medium for presenting the children's work which is wholly acceptable to their peers. They provide many opportunities for discussion, for reading and written work, and for using any special abilities the children may have. Above all, they provide opportunities for success.

It should be emphasized that extensive technical knowledge and equipment are not vital to such a project. The simplest way of working is often the most effective, because the children want to see themselves on the screen as rapidly as possible. When the children had made up a story in outline, we shot it scene by scene (outside, because we had no special lighting) and looked at it critically, discussing what we had done before re-shooting it, or going on to the next scene.

When we showed the film to other children, they gazed in amazement at their friends on the screen, and asked 'Is it true? Did it happen?' Parents who had never made contact with the teachers were pressed by their children to come and see the children on the screen, and they came. (It is surely very understandable that they were readier to come to see their children's triumphs than to discuss their problems and failures.) The relationship which develops between the teacher and the children in a project of this kind, when they are all working together, all making mistakes and helping each other to put them right, is in itself worth the extra time and work involved for the teacher. It is essential for the children to be able to regard mistakes as a normal and inevitable part of learning and to accept them as such. A school should be a place where one can make mistakes (*in other words, learn*) safely, learning at the same time how to correct them. If the mistakes can be cut out before the finished product is shown to others outside the group, as is normal practice in the adult world, it helps the children to gain the success and approval they need so much.

One way of building up one's own 'self-image' is to do things to help other people. Backward children are so often on the receiving end. They rarely have an opportunity of giving service to others who need their help, and if it is possible to arrange this kind of experience for them, it can be of real value. Singing carols in a hospital at Christmas is one example of such an activity. Being asked to help younger children is another.

The teacher has to consider the situation as she finds it, recognize her own and the children's abilities and limitations, and use whatever opportunities arise or can be created.

d DEVELOPING NEW ATTITUDES TOWARDS READING

If it is important to encourage a climate of literacy among children in an infant school, it is even more essential to create a way of life in a remedial class in which reading is seen as a skill worth the effort of acquiring, and which is moreover within the children's reach: late starters need to see reading as part of their lives, and they need early success.

Remedial teachers often try to link reading to any known interest a child may have: he begins by making a book about cars, or aeroplanes, or astronauts and spaceships, about dogs or pigeons or whatever topic he finds interesting. Older children seem less ready than younger ones to make books about themselves—to do so might perhaps lay them open to criticism or comparisons with their fellows.

This is clearly one way of involving the children in reading. Another is to make reading a part of other activities going on in the classroom, as the teacher does with younger children. Some older children may find the skill important to them because it has a direct bearing on the development of other interests: they want to make a model, and need to be able to read the instructions; they want to cook, and need to be able to read a recipe. Reading is connected with so many activities, that it can be linked with any interest the child may have.

As with younger children, the whole setting of the classroom is important in developing such interests, in providing illustrations and materials which help children to learn the meanings of words and provide them with factual information and stimulus for thinking and using words.

Illustrative material is especially important for older children who cannot read. The child's only way of finding things out independently, if he cannot read, is through observation. Interesting visual presentation of facts and ideas is particularly important for him. The very fact that the classroom is an interesting place, and that he and his interests have a share in everything to be found there, is valuable.

Some of the activities used in infant schools to encourage speech and writing can be developed with older children. Instead of telling their news, the children might write it on a piece of paper. The teacher checks this, and the children re-write it if necessary. It is then stuck up on a big sheet of coloured paper pinned to the wall. (The sheet should be changed regularly—an important point.) I shall always remember two items from such a wall-newspaper which I saw in a junior school. The first said: 'The policeman who used to see us across the road has turned into a detective.' The second read: 'Peter has rabbits for sale. 2/6 your own pick. 2/- Peter's pick.' This newspaper was clearly one the children wrote and read themselves. It was alive with their interests. Such a newspaper could be developed into a news-sheet circulated by the class to others in the school, with all the opportunities for reading and writing which would inevitably arise in its production, and the kudos of being the publishers would enhance the status of the remedial group.

If a child seems to have few or no interests outside school, then it may be possible for the teacher to encourage their development within the classroom. Something which is alive usually rates high among such activities, so it is worth the effort to try to keep some creatures in the classroom. Looking after an animal has the added value to the backward child that it is a situation in which he is the one who is able to do things, the one in control, and this is an experience he rarely has. It is very necessary, of course, for the teacher to carry the final responsibility for the animal's welfare and to remember that children who have had a rough time themselves may be aggressive in their turn to weaker creatures, human or animal. If the animal suffers, either through neglect or attack, the harm done is to the child as well as to the creature. But a genuine interest of this kind can provide invaluable opportunities for developing language through discussion and through written captions and instructions, as well as for encouraging compassionate and responsible behaviour.

Other areas of learning offer opportunities too. Any craft the child learns, any collection of objects which he makes, provides a setting for spoken and written words based on immediate experience which underlines and reinforces their meaning.

Reading aloud to the children

But factual material, even if it is about something in which the children are interested, is not enough. The development of imagination and imaginative experience remains a vital part of reading. It is a part of the interpretation of words, even if these are no more than a recipe for making a cake; but it is only through an imaginative response to stories and descriptions that children can learn to think about and to widen their own experience, to see beyond their own immediate environment, and to enter into the new worlds they can find in books. Unless the teacher reads descriptions, stories and poetry to the class, children who cannot read may miss everything books have to offer. There is one very marked difference by the age of about seven or eight between most children who can read relatively easily anything which interests them and those who cannot: it is in the amount of time they spend in reading. Those who read well practise every day by reading, reinforcing all they have learned; those who find reading difficult begin to avoid situations in which they have to struggle with printed words. The teacher can help to bridge the gap in imaginative experience which results from this by reading to the children, though only success in learning to read will encourage them to choose to read in their own time.

Reading aloud is therefore even more important than it is for the teacher of younger children. Many of the children may come from homes where books are never read, and their only experience of books is in school. Reading aloud factual accounts and information from books is also important. If the teacher omits this, she cannot demonstrate the importance of checking opinion against fact, and in referring to such books she shows her own respect for truth, and indicates the means of forming independent opinions, as well as how to find out something one wants to know.

Television, pictures, charts, visual aids of all kinds, do not replace reading, they supplement it, providing material for imaginative use. In the last resort, each of us creates his own world through his response to all he sees and hears and all that happens to him. In teaching children to read, helping them to use their experience and imagination to understand the text is as important as decoding. The effort of learning basic skills may absorb most of their energies when they are just beginning to read for themselves, but this is all the more reason for reading *to* them at this stage, so that sometimes the basic decoding is done for them, and their minds are free to think and to imagine.

In this way, too, they can gain familiarity with patterns of written English. They learn, through listening, the patterns of language they will meet later in reading for themselves. The farther their own speech is from the standard English of books, the more such reading will help them to become familiar with the written language.

We can help to stimulate the children's imagination by the way we read. It is worthwhile preparing and thinking about the book or story beforehand from this point of view. Able children, who read a great many books themselves, can sometimes turn even the dull reading of a text into something alive in their own minds. Children without this experience need all the help which effective reading aloud can give. A semi-dramatic presentation is often a stimulating one, when the reader conveys the character of the people in the story by voice and perhaps slight change of position or gesture. (It is easy to check whether the reading is effective or not by, awareness of the children's response.)

Tape-recordings and records

But not all teachers can read aloud well, though this is a skill to be developed. This is where tape-recordings and records can be useful. There are many series of poems on records, and if a teacher is uninterested in poetry herself, or cannot read it well aloud, at least she can give the children the opportunity of hearing it, just as the teacher uninterested in music, or unable to play any instrument, can still play a record. But recordings have a value of their own. They can stimulate imagination through the use of different voices, through dramatic presentation (with a narrator if necessary), or through sound effects. Some stories and poems are more effective if read by a man, some by a woman. No teacher can be both. (Remedial classes are often taken by women, because they have experience in teaching younger children to read. This may mean that children in a remedial class have never been taught by a man, and they enjoy hearing a man read. It is a new experience for them.)

If no records or tapes are available of the particular stories needed, other members of staff, friends or even a local dramatic society may often co-operate in providing one.

Such recordings help not only to create the background of the story, to bring the characters to life, but also provide a starting point for discussions, in which the children learn to think about the content of what they are listening to, to question ideas, to put their own thoughts into words. Misconceptions come to light, and the teacher has an opportunity to clear these up and to explain the meanings of new words.

Tape-recordings of stories in the children's readers, using the text of the book as closely as possible but perhaps providing an introductory story and sound effects to help it to come alive, serve the useful purpose of making the books the children are able to read for themselves, simple as these may be, part of the whole idea of reading being presented to them. Such a recording made by adults may be used as a stimulus for the children to make their own, using the texts of their readers. (This incidentally provides much practice in reading and re-reading words they already know, in dramatic form.) If it transpires that they find some of the stories and characters laughable or unreal, no matter. To be able to discover the emptiness of a text is sometimes as important as discovering deeper meaning; they can develop such stories to provide something which is real to them, or to provide farcical situations. It can also be a stimulus to making up and perhaps writing more interesting or dramatic stories themselves.

Models

Making a model of the background of a story may help children to visualize it, and perhaps to invent other stories with a similar background for themselves. The photograph plate VI shows the strange planet made by a group of children whose readers were based on science fiction. Again the actual making of the model not only provides opportunities for discussion, for clarifying the meanings of words, and for children who have special skills to contribute; it can also be used to stimulate ideas for original work.

Reading is a vital skill, but although this must be recognized with a group of backward children it does not mean that it should occupy the whole of their school lives to the exclusion of other areas of learning, for these provide the essential experience on which vocabulary may be built, as well as opportunities for success. Modelling and carpentry, painting and creative work of all kinds are particularly important for children who have limited verbal skills, as ways of expressing thought and imagination. Every part of the school day can contribute to the teaching of reading, even when the connection is not apparent to the superficial observer, and it will certainly not all consist of specific exercises with books and printed words. But it is wise to set aside part of each day for systematic teaching. When they are succeeding, children welcome the feeling that they are making steady regular progress, even if the progress is slow.

e SYSTEMATIC TEACHING OF EARLY READING SKILLS

It is sometimes argued that a complete change of method is helpful in teaching older children who have hitherto failed to learn to read. This argument recognizes that one of the most difficult problems to be overcome is the child's own attitude, the barrier to learning built up by past failure, which results in such avoidance of any reading situation, that, if presented with a book or printed or written words, he 'closes up' and withdraws all attention and effort. The methods used in teaching him in the past have hitherto failed. On both counts a different method, so the argument runs, is more likely to succeed.

But the position is rarely as simple as this. There are some skills which are necessary in any reading situation: learning to recognize familiar words and groups of words quickly and without conscious analysis is one of them; a method of attack on new or unfamiliar words is another; discovering the probable meaning of an unknown word from its context is a third. There are many others. Children have their individual strengths and weaknesses and it is only common sense to use their special abilities to the full in teaching, so that if a child has a good visual memory this might suggest visual methods of teaching a basic sight vocabulary, whereas a child with a very poor visual memory might need a different approach; but for effective reading, both children will in the end come to recognize some words at a glance. A child who distinguishes, hears and remembers sounds readily may learn by predominantly phonic methods much more quickly than another who seems unable to hear, let alone blend, sounds. But phonic clues are so useful in reading a word which will be recognized if it can be spoken, that it may be wise to spend time in helping the second child to listen and learn some phoneme/grapheme relationships even though visual methods predominate.

Further, even a child who is unable to read anything his teacher gives him, may already have acquired some skills which will be useful: he may even be a slow developer, who is emerging from the pre-reading stage with experiences and spoken vocabulary only just at the point when systematic teaching of specific skills can be effective. He may have missed these in the infant school, not because they did not occur but because he had not yet reached a stage when he could profit by them.

One should take into consideration everything one knows about a child in planning how to teach him to read, but one thing which every teacher discovers is that she always has questions about a child to which she does not know the answers; she has to begin teaching him nonetheless, adapting and revising her methods as she goes along according to his response. The teacher herself may use some methods more effectively and imaginatively than others and although she should always attempt to be flexible and follow up any indications that a child responds more readily to one approach rather than another, the teacher's own belief in, and enthusiasm for, any particular method of teaching reading is often an important factor in a child's success. Confidence is catching and a child who has hitherto failed needs all the confidence he can acquire in his teacher and her ways of doing things.

But there are differences in teaching older children the beginnings of reading. As they grow older, our relationship with the children changes and their own response to adults and to their contemporaries alters. In teaching older children who have failed so far to learn to read, it is often helpful to take them at least part way into one's confidence: to tell them, for example, that a game will help them to learn more new words, or in simple terms to explain (or better still let them discover for themselves through experience) the alphabetic principle in words, that certain letters stand for certain spoken sounds, at a rather earlier stage in reading than one would with younger children. (There is a very good example of how this may be done in *The Quality of Learning* by Ronald Morris, and the games in *Stott's Programmed Reading Kit* provide ways in which older children can, through experience, discover principles for themselves.) It may be helpful, too, to give the children a possible explanation for their past failure. If a child realizes that he has had special difficulty in learning in the past for some reason outside his control (eg because he needed glasses, or was away from school at a crucial period or frequently absent with minor ailments, or because he changed schools a number of times, or some such reason), it can help to restore his self-respect and his confidence in his ability to learn, now that the situation is different. It shifts the burden of responsibility for not having learned off his own shoulders. It is a human weakness to try to blame something outside ourselves for our failures, but a child's inability to read at an early age can hardly be regarded, even by those who abhor excuses, as his own fault: to find some cause in past circumstances may result in giving renewed hope, and in the child making a renewed effort to learn.

(i) METHODS AND TECHNIQUES

Some children who have not yet learned to read by the time they enter the junior school may have such specific difficulties that they need remedial teaching by special methods. Every teacher has a responsibility to notice such children and alert the appropriate services, co-operating with them as much as she can. But there will be many other children who can be taught to read by methods already described in the earlier part of this book, provided that these are adapted for use with older children.

Establishing a basic sight vocabulary and learning new words

The book made by himself is as useful a bridge for an older child between the general climate of literacy and systematic teaching as it is for a younger one. It may be even more important, in its implicit indication of his teacher's concern for him and his interests. The teacher is going out to meet him more than half way. But the older boy (or girl) may well be dissatisfied with his own drawings as illustrations, unless they happen to be better than average. He is much more likely to find illustrations cut from magazines or newspapers acceptable. Postcards, or sheets of transfers, often make acceptable illustrations, and provide ideas for the book.

Photographs, taken by the teacher or the children, are another useful source of illustrations. These may be of the children themselves, or of their pets, models, or any other objects which they want to include. Children find photographs of places and objects seen on an expedition interesting: photographs of the children discovering such places seem to be irresistible, as if they saw nothing more remarkable in the world than themselves.

An old typewriter can be a most useful piece of apparatus when it comes to providing a text, either for a book, an item for a wall-newspaper, or any other short written work which will be seen by others, especially at the secondary level. If the boy or girl first writes down what he wants to say as well as he can and then takes it to the teacher, who corrects it with him (or sometimes perhaps to another child in the class, who is appointed editor by virtue of his reading and writing skills), he can then type out the corrected version to go with the illustrations. It cannot be too often emphasized that mistakes are a normal part of learning. In this situation they provide the teacher with a useful indication of places where specific teaching is needed.

Reading games are useful, both to establish a sight vocabulary and to teach phonics to older children. As with younger children, they provide a setting in which practice is acceptable and they break down isolation in learning. Older children often particularly enjoy working in groups. A boy who has begun to learn to read can sometimes take charge of a group game played by others who are at an earlier stage, and in doing so he not only achieves status, but also revises earlier learning in a way acceptable to him. Teaching someone else is an effective method of learning.

For establishing a basic sight vocabulary, games based on words, or words and matching pictures, are useful; games based on some kind of quest can be adapted to very simple reading levels, and most children enjoy them. If there are children in the class who can print and draw reasonably well, there is no reason why they should not make up the cards for themselves or others. It will give them useful extra practice in studying words. Alternatively, an older class might make them for younger children.

Matching games

'Matching Threes' is a simple example of such a game, which can be used with any reading scheme. Make a list of words which can readily be illustrated and which the children are likely to meet frequently in their reading. Using this, make a pack of 50-60 cards, in which there is one picture-card and two word-cards for each noun, eg

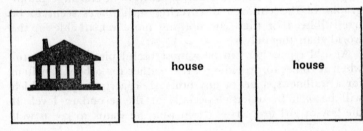

Each player is dealt five cards. The rest of the pack is put face down on the table. The top card is turned up and placed beside the pack. The player to the left of the dealer begins. He picks up a card (either from the top of the pack or the card lying beside it) and discards a card, placing it face-upwards. If he has a complete matching three (picture-card and two word-cards) he puts it down and takes three more cards from the pack, making his hand up to five again. The next player then has a turn and so on, until the whole pack has been used. When the pack has been run through once, the residual cards are shuffled and used again. The player with the most matching-threes wins.

Journey or Quest games

On a large oblong of cardboard draw out a track and mark it in squares. At intervals along the track, make distinctive squares by using a different colour (or symbol). Prepare a number of cards of simple directions for the journey, using words from the vocabulary of the reading material.*

The players begin at the square marked 'start' and continue to the square marked 'end', but whenever they land on the distinctive squares, they have to read a card and do whatever it says. In addition, natural hazards may be marked on the board, or the players may collect various objects as they go along, the names of the objects being printed on or beside certain squares, and the objects themselves pictured on cards to be collected from a 'bank'.

There is one danger to be watched for in using any games with children who have experienced frequent failure: it is that success in the game may matter too much. If a game is played with a teacher (as it may be in a remedial situation) the problem is avoidable, because the teacher can usually arrange things so that she often loses, but when it is played between children, the winner may enjoy it but the loser can be quite disproportionately upset, because any kind of success is so rare that it matters very much even to win a game. For this reason it is wise to base games at least partly on chance,

---

* These should be in short sentences, using words from the vocabulary of the early readers, key words, or other words which will be important in the basic reading vocabulary of the children eg for children using *Griffin Pirate Stories*: The ship is on the rocks. Go back to the island.

rather than skill, to give everyone an opportunity of winning, and to watch carefully to make sure no individual always wins or always loses.

It should be remembered, too, that games, although they have their place, are not reading in the full sense of the term, and cannot replace books.

Other devices for establishing a sight vocabulary

Games are useful, but learning does not need to be disguised as fun. Once they see the purpose of what they are asked to do and realize that they can achieve it, many children will welcome various kinds of word study designed to help them.

A simple method for remembering new words which some-times works with a child who has a poor visual memory is to ask him to look at the word, copy it, cover it up and try to write it from memory, checking his attempt with the original and continuing until he can do it.

The children keep a pack of cards of words they know, to be checked frequently with a partner—either a child who can read the words, or, in the case of nouns, with another child at the same reading level who has an illustrated list of the same words. The advantage of the first arrangement is that the partner is given recognition as a good reader, and asked to use his skill to help someone else; the advantage of the second type of partnership is that both children are learning and revising the words together. Provided the number of known words increases day by day, the growing size of the pack of cards demonstrates his progress to the child.

This demonstration is important. It means that he can measure his learning, and realize that he is succesful. A simple histogram may help to make the progress explicit. All that is needed is a sheet of squared paper. Every time he reads the words on the cards, he colours in the appropriate number of squares in columns across the page indicating the growing number of words he can recognize out of context. (After a time, one square of a given colour may have to stand for ten words.)

Such devices are, of course, only useful when the child is succeeding: they demonstrate to him that he can learn.

Individual picture dictionaries or personal word-books arranged alphabetically may help to establish a basic vocabulary at a later stage, and teach the order of letters incidentally at the same time.

Other basic skills

Learning words, either through games or in some other form of word-study, is not the same thing as reading. It is an important adjunct to books, because, especially in the early stages, all the necessary practice in word recognition can scarcely be given through books without making the text too banal; but the link with books needs to be made and activities demanding reading in the fullest sense of interpreting the meaning of the printed words are very important. As soon as a child reaches a level when simple books can be read, there should be every opportunity for reading: sometimes an activity may follow from this, but opportunities simply to read and enjoy an imaginative or factual text within his level of reading ability are vital. As many books as possible which are at the interest level of the children, but which are at or below their reading age, should be available, with time set aside 'just' for reading. As with younger children, such books may sometimes be read by the teacher to the class, with all the skill an adult has to bring the text to life.

Some systematic teaching of phonics usually has an important part to play in helping older children learn to read, partly because it is an important skill in unlocking the meaning of new words, and partly because it can give a child the feeling that he is making steady progress, that he has a way of attacking a new word, of 'operating effectively'. D H Stott makes a point which is very pertinent here: 'What really motivates learning? The normal human being ... likes to be in a position where he is operating effectively—keeping his end up, controlling his environment and arranging it to suit him, learning more about it so that he understands how to control it ... The need is for progressive effectiveness.'

Children who reach the secondary school unable to read are often acutely aware of this as a disability, no matter what attitude they adopt to cover it up. If the teacher can convince them that they can learn and she can teach them to read, some may respond better to straight teaching than to an approach through games. Specific teaching is more effective if it is done regularly, does not last too long, is seen to be effective and is quickly put to use in other situations.

Cartoon books

Older children enjoy simple humour; the fact that children who have acquired only the simplest reading skills enjoy a good story may be seen in their interest in comics, where most of the story is carried by the pictures. Suppose, for example, that a group of children was still at the stage of learning initial consonants, short vowel sounds and simple combinations of these. A short teaching period of a few minutes each day could be followed by making a cartoon strip, or book on similar lines. This might be begun as a class or group activity: the name of the characters might be Tim Mud or Pat Pin, and their adventures shown in a series of pictures of pin men, easily drawn even by those (teachers or children) who have very limited graphic skills. (Such pictures are very quickly drawn too, on the blackboard, or on sheets of paper, and the amount of time spent on them is not disproportionate to the amount of time spent on the text, as it might be with more elaborate illustrations.) A simple caption is printed underneath, whenever it is needed to supplement the action. The names of the characters, and (if the teacher is working with the group) the choice of words in the captions may include as large a number of short, regular words as possible.

Another advantage of this kind of activity is that key words (the words used most frequently in any printed material) are bound by their very nature to be frequently introduced and repeated. A teacher who has the list of most frequently used words in mind can see that they are incorporated in the text, even if they are not (as they are likely to be) all included in the captions suggested by the children. The words are then set in a context which makes their meaning clear and a situation is created in which the children can see the point when the teacher says: 'Look: we are using this word all the time, but some of you are still not sure of it. Let's look at it carefully and really learn it.' Not only looking is involved: the children are listening to sounds, noticing phoneme/grapheme relationships, watching the teacher write the sentences and words, and writing them themselves.

Groups of children and individuals can of course make such stories on their own: the teacher need not always work with them. They are particularly useful for children whose skills are so limited that they are unable to write the whole story in words. Scenes and incidents which are important for the story, but which could not be written down without a great deal of labour and adult help, can be quickly shown graphically; but words are so useful that the children realize that even one or two may help to make the meaning clear, and the proportion of text to pictures can be gradually increased with increasing skills.

Songs

Songs are another useful source of reading material, particularly if the children know the words by heart. If these are printed on a large chart, or written on the blackboard, and the teacher (or a child who can read) runs a pointer along the lines while the children are singing, the words become familiar, and their duration in time is also clear.

Kinaesthetic methods

Kinaesthetic methods may also prove effective. It sometimes helps children to trace over letters or words, as well as to copy or write them. The Marion Richardson system of writing was introduced as far back as the nineteen thirties, and while there are arguments for children learning to print before they learn to write, the method has two features specially helpful in teaching reading: the children begin by making continuous writing patterns running from left to right, which not only give them practice in left to right orientation, but help them to develop rhythmic movements; and there are cards of rhymes and poems which the children can trace. These patterns, or similar ones invented by the children, can be used decoratively, eg to make frames for mounting illustrations (the work need not be dull or formal) and can be useful even if some other system of writing or printing is being taught.

(ii) USING READING SCHEMES WITH OLDER CHILDREN

All the arguments for using a graded reading scheme set out in Chapter 3 are still valid in teaching older children, with perhaps the additional one that the teacher fresh from college in the junior or secondary school may have even less experience and training specifically in the teaching of reading than the beginner in the infant school. With older children who have had difficulty in reading, it is even more important to build up the imaginary world of the stories outside the books themselves, and this can be more easily organized where one scheme is used for the main part of the teaching, although of course this should not exclude other books for supplementary reading. Whichever reading scheme is chosen, it should be one that is new to the children: the feeling of a fresh start is important. The content of the books should be acceptable to the children, ie the stories should be at their interest level and above all the illustrations should show characters with whom they can identify without loss of self-regard. (Pictures of five- and six-year-old children are to be avoided in books used with juniors and still more with secondary school children.) The characters in the stories need not be the same age as the reader: children never seem to find any difficulty in identifying themselves with Robin Hood or other adventurers, and at the junior school age folk-tale/fairy-tale characters or animal heroes are often acceptable. The guiding principle seems to be that at least the main character and the majority of people in the story should be of the same age or older than the reader, or of an apparently different order of beings. At the same time, the level of reading difficulty should be appropriate to the child's reading age or, to begin with, a little below it.

The importance of initial success

Initial success in the first book he meets in his new school or class is of very great importance. For children who have failed to learn any important skill, the value of success in some part of their lives has already been discussed. If newly won confidence in some other activity is re-inforced by success in reading the first book of a new scheme, the barrier to learning may be at least temporarily broken: if the success continues, no matter how slowly, a child's whole attitude can change. At the very least, he will find reading more acceptable and the effort to learn more worth making. It is important to choose a reading scheme which has many books at the earliest levels and where the gradient of difficulty is not too steep, and for this reason, too, pre-readers and early books in a reading scheme should be short, and arranged so that a child can hardly fail to read them. The first pre-reader of the *Griffin Pirate Stories*, for example, is more like a picture dictionary than a connected story: the full background story of the red pirate may be read to the children from the handbook (or they can listen to the tape-recording), but the first book they read is so simple that they can guess the words from the pictures. Teaching them to recognize the words and phrases comes after they have had the experience of reading a whole book and the reassurance which comes from being able to do this. Single words accompany the pictures, as well as a phrase or a sentence which contains them. In this way, the child's attention is drawn to the single word, though it is read first in context. It helps to indicate that phrases and sentences are made up of separate words. (The same idea is used in the introductory books to *One, Two, Three and Away!*, in the earliest books of *Dominoes* and in some other reading schemes.) Older children must learn the same skills as the younger ones, but the content of the books has to be adapted to their interests.

Anticipating difficulties

It is also important to have available any ancillary games and apparatus which may go with the books. These will have been designed not only to provide essential practice to reinforce the vocabulary and skills acquired through reading the books, but also may include 'bridging games', exercises and other activities which anticipate vocabulary and language skills needed, so that difficulties are met and overcome *before the child encounters them in the next book in the series*. For example, *Looking for Jewels* is a bridging game from the Pirate Reading Scheme. In Book 4 of the *Griffin Pirate Stories*, one of the pirates goes off to look for jewels: rubies, emeralds and sapphires. These are three words which the children are unlikely to recognize immediately in print, and which the teacher cannot be sure will be part of their spoken vocabulary. This is the time for the teacher to gather together the group of children who have just finished (or are still reading) Book 3. She might initiate questions and discussion by showing them a ring or a brooch set with 'jewels' (Woolworth's jewellery is often large and shining), or a picture of a crown or open treasure chest. The teacher introduces the words rubies, emeralds and sapphires into the discussion, and perhaps writes them on the blackboard. She then introduces the bridging game, which on this occasion is a 'quest' game, in which each player sets out with a little ship along a route marked on a pictorial map, collecting rubies, emeralds and sapphires as he goes along. (The jewels to be collected are part of the materials of the game.) By the time they have played it once or twice, the names of the jewels are part of the children's spoken vocabulary, and many of them can recognize the printed words too. A story from the Pirate Handbook reinforces this learning, and introduces Book 4, which the children will now find much easier to read than they would have done if they had gone straight to it from Book 3.

This type of bridging game, and the teaching which goes with it, can be adapted and used with many reading series. If they are not part of the ancillary apparatus available with a scheme, it is well worthwhile to make bridging games and collect other useful materials which introduce the vocabulary of new books.

Games are only one way of reducing the gradient of difficulty. Again, a short period of specific teaching *anticipating* new words, ideas and sentences, is often more effective than waiting until the children become bogged down in unfamiliar material. It is partly to arrange for this kind of anticipation of difficulties that a teacher makes a plan of the books in a reading scheme, noting the points at which special teaching will clearly be particularly helpful. The reading scheme itself provides a framework for teaching.

'Readers' in serial form

Although it is useful to have a number of simple books on different themes as supplementary readers, there are advantages in having a series of stories about the same characters in the main reading scheme. Children like series in which they meet the same people—one has only to look at their comics and at the television programmes they watch to realize this. When the text of the earliest books must inevitably be slight, depth of character and richness of background can only be built up very gradually. *Hamlet* cannot be written in twenty different words and sixteen pages. If the same characters are met in a number of books they can be developed into something rather more than cardboard figures and the setting of the stories can be gradually filled in, while the vocabulary burden remains one which a child struggling to learn to read can carry. In other words, the gap between 'readers' and 'books' can be lessened, perhaps even bridged. Older children who still need graded reading material should have stories which are as close to real books as possible even more than children in the infant school, if they are to maintain a belief that reading has something to offer them through the long process of learning the skill.

If a reading scheme is in the form of a serial, and each book is an episode in the whole story, a further incentive to reading can be built into the books. The problem of encouraging the slow reader to practise his skill has already been mentioned. If the book he reads ends in a cliff-hanger situation, so that he finds that he actually wants to go on to the next book to find out what happens, the incentive for further reading exists in the book itself. Intrinsic motivation lasts longer as a force for learning and action than motivation which has to be engendered from outside. Of course this is a double-edged solution to the problem of encouraging the children to read: if they don't find the story interesting, the last thing they want is more books on the same theme. But the chances are that the story will be more interesting if the writer has had a little more room than a first 'reader' can give him to develop the theme and the teacher has had the opportunity to help the children create an imaginary world from activities alongside the books.

I should like to conclude this chapter by stressing the importance of encouraging each child to feel that he has a contribution to make to the work of the group. To make a recognized individual contribution to a joint project is to achieve a recognized status, and this is what so many backward children need.

Readers of books about experiments in educaton often find a reference to the 'Hawthorne effect'. The name comes from an experiment carried out many years ago at the Hawthorne Works of the General Electric Company at Chicago. The conditions under which a group of girls assembled telephone relays were changed, to see whether such alterations would improve output. The girls had at the beginning no pauses for rest and they worked a 48-hour week. They were first of all given piecework, whereupon output went up. They were given five minute rest-pauses, and output went up again. When the rest-pauses were lengthened to ten minutes, it went up still more, and when they were given a free meal and allowed to leave half an hour earlier than usual, output again increased. As a final experiment, all the improvements were removed and for three months the girls went back to the old conditions before the experiment began. During this final period output was higher than it had ever been before.*

* See the account of this experiment in *The Social Psychology of Industry*, by J A C Brown.

The explanation put forward for the results of this experiment was that the attitude of the girls had changed, and that it was this which led to increased productivity. The girls felt that they were important. They were no longer just work-hands: they had been asked by the company to take part in the experiment, in order to find the best working conditions. They knew what they were doing and why, and felt themselves to be valued members of the firm. The 'Hawthorne effect', ie the increase in effort and effectiveness which occurs when people feel themselves to be doing something interesting and worthwhile and in which their willing participation is important and recognized, has to be allowed for in assessing the results of educational experiments, eg those carried out with i.t.a. The teachers taking part in such experiments may unconsciously react like the girls in the Hawthorne Works and, without meaning to, or realizing what is happening, become more effective as teachers simply because they regard their work and themselves as an important part of the whole project. The application to the children we teach is also clear. If those children feel themselves to be working for an agreed purpose, in partnership with their teachers, with a recognized part to play as valued members of the group, their output and effectiveness is likely to increase also.

Anecdotes are not evidence, but this point was once summed up for me so simply by a boy in a secondary modern school, that it is worth repeating. Peter (not his real name) was in his last term. When he first went to school, at the age of eleven, he had been unable to read and he had attended a remedial centre twice a week for two years. At the centre, his teacher (a man) had included him in a group who had done all kinds of interesting things: they had made a simple film, they had been on expeditions, and his teacher, who was himself very good at woodwork, had helped him make various things. I was in the school working with a small group of eleven-year-olds, trying out some new reading materials. We had found refuge in a corner of a quiet attic, which was also used for storing books. We were working together round a table, trying out a reading game, when Peter came in to fetch a book. He nodded to me, cast an appraising glance over the table, fetched his book and went back to the door. Just before closing it behind him, he turned and made a pronouncement: 'The trouble with boys as can't read,' he said, 'is that teachers isn't interested in 'em.' And with that he left. As a statement about teachers, it was considerably less than fair: many teachers spend hours of their free time attending courses, reading books about methods, and doing their best to help just those children. But as a statement of the way the children sometimes feel, and as a key to the first step in remedial treatment, it goes right to the heart of the matter. Even an inexperienced teacher can feel encouraged. If the teacher really is keenly interested in the children and in helping them to learn to read, the children respond.

NOTES ON BOOKS FOR FURTHER READING

As this book has stressed, many of the suggestions for teaching reading in the infant school can be used for older children if they are adapted to their needs and interests, so the books already mentioned in earlier notes for further reading are useful for a teacher of children who have reading difficulties. In fact, they provide an essential background of knowledge against which any special suggestions for remedial teaching should be set.

The following books deal specifically with children who have failed to learn to read in the infant school:

Ablewhite, R C (1967) *The Slow Reader* Heinemann Educational Books. This is concerned chiefly with children at the secondary level.
Ravenette, A T (1968) *Dimensions of Reading Difficulties* Pergamon.
Tansley, A E (1967) *Reading and Remedial Reading* Routledge and Kegan Paul.

The Pirate Reading Scheme Handbook (ie the manual for the Griffin and Dragon Pirate Stories) describes how the principles underlying the teaching practices suggested here are worked out in detail in all the books and ancillary materials of a specific reading scheme.

Some books intended primarily for teachers in special schools contain chapters on the teaching of reading which are helpful for those in ordinary schools, too. These include *The Education of Slow Learning Children* by Tansley and Gulliford and *Basic Teaching for Slow Learners*, by Peter Bell.

Reading and its Difficulties, by M D Vernon (Cambridge University Press, 1971) is a comprehensive, detailed and scholarly survey of the whole problem, based on current research findings, but it is a book for those who already have some knowledge of the subject. It has a very complete list of references.

It should be noted that the University of Reading *Centre for the Teaching of Reading Brochures* include an up-to-date list of *Reading Schemes for Slow Learners.*

The Social Psychology of Industry, by J A C Brown, not only contains a summary of the Hawthorne experiment referred to on page 117, but also many stimulating ideas and comments about human beings and the way in which they respond Although the book is primarily about people in industry, nc teacher will have any difficulty in seeing the relevance of what is said to work in the classroom and the life of the school.

PART FOUR

Developing Reading Skills

7

After the beginning

One way of learning to teach effectively, is to learn a new skill at one's own level, and watch closely how one learns. To do so is to become aware of sudden spurts forward, of plateau periods when no progress seems to be made at all, of the results of practice, of emotonal reactions to praise and blame, to success and failure. Generally speaking, teachers are people who themselves had little if any difficulty in learning to read. The insight into the learning process which comes from introspection while learning a new skill oneself can be a very useful complement to reading the results of research, in helping one to understand children's learning and failure to learn.

Suppose, for example, that you are learning to drive a car. You already have a good deal of experience to draw on, from seeing cars in traffic and from travelling in them, watching other people drive. Motivation for learning is strong. But neither of these things is enough, especially if the car is an old one which demands a considerable degree of technical competence: some degree of systematic teaching and practice is necessary too.

The first stages are often exciting, as you feel yourself in control in a new situation. To begin with you learn quickly many new skills—to steer, to change gear, to brake, to accelerate. During this period, the situation in which you are learning must be simplified as much as possible, so that you can concentrate on the basic skills, and make safely the mistakes which are an inevitable part of learning. So your teacher chooses the quietest and straightest country road to be found, or even a private road where you can be sure of encountering no other traffic. Your whole attention is so absorbed by the sheer management of the mechanics of driving, that you have little left over for anything else, though you remain aware of the rewards of being able to drive.

It is only when you can handle the car without having to think consciously how to manipulate the wheel, the gear lever, the clutch and the brake that you can really begin to learn to manoeuvre it in normal driving conditions, although the two to some extent go together. You can only learn how to make a hill-start by practising on a hill, and when to brake as well as how to brake by driving on ordinary roads and in traffic.

Using your new skills in handling the car in traffic is nonetheless a new stage, and at this point you have many more things to learn about the placing of your own car and the movements of other cars and people. It is only when you have reached a certain level of competence that you have attention available to notice road signs and markings. You have to learn when and how to pass other cars, and when not to; to allow for other people's actions. At this point, you can learn by watching someone else drive, as well as by driving yourself, especially if you are consciously noticing how things are done. Although you can now drive in the more difficult conditions of traffic, it is wise to spend time on quiet country roads as well, where skills can be consolidated and made less conscious through practice, confidence increased, and the feeling developed of what it is really like to drive a car.

At a still later stage, you have to learn to work out and follow a route through new country, and it is only when you are really experienced that you can drive a car competently, find your way, and at the same time engage in intelligent conversation with your passengers.

It is worth noticing, too, that at certain times you may revert to an earlier stage. If you are trying to follow a complicated route through a city you do not know, you may be unable to join in a general conversation and you may even miss road signs that you would otherwise have noticed, such as an unusual speed limit sign. When driving in icy conditions, your whole attention may be directed to the handling of the car, the sheer mechanical skills necessary to keep it on the road. Such skills are then by no means wholly unconscious.

This pattern of learning is not dissimilar to that in learning other skills, including the skill of reading. Both are really a complex of skills: in both, attention is directed at first to skills which will later become largely subconscious, unless something occurs (complicated or bad road conditions, or a difficult piece of reading or an unknown word) which brings them temporarily to the fore.

When children are beginning to learn to read, they have inevitably to concentrate on recognizing words or on decoding. It is only when they are able to free their attention from these that they can begin to learn other reading skills. This does not mean that the content of their earliest books is unimportant. It is very important indeed, because it helps them to understand what reading is about, what it has to to offer to them. Having spent a little time working out the caption to a picture which interests them, they can always re-read it and, now that they can recognize the words more easily, think about their meaning. (One of the advantages of 'dramatic readers' using the same text as the book, is the opportunity they offer to go over the text again, when it has already been closely studied, with a mind free to concentrate on interpretation because the text is familiar.) It does mean that there is much more to teach children about reading than basic skills of word recognition and decoding.

There is another analogy between reading and learning to drive which may usefully be made. Even an experienced driver can look at the scenery and think about things other than driving most easily when he is going along a straight, empty road. If we want children to think about what they are reading, to connect it with their own lives, to build up in their minds the imaginary worlds unfolded in the book and people them with the characters of the story, then either the text should be one which is well within their reading ability as regards the mechanics of reading (ie the words used, the length and structure of the sentences, must be familiar to them); or else the text must be read *to* them, so that their minds are freed from having to interpret the print, and they can listen (using language skills so familiar that they are unaware of them) and think about the meaning of what they hear. Both these situations are useful to the teacher who is encouraging the development of reading skills.

As soon as the children can recognize the commoner words, and can use picture and contextual clues and have available simple phonic skills to unlock new words, they need as wide a variety of books at the early reading levels as possible. When a child has completed Book 1 of a reading scheme, Book 2 in the same scheme may be a good deal easier for him to read than Book 1 of another set of readers. But by the time he has reached Book 3 or 4 (depending on how the books are graded and the teaching methods used), he can probably manage books from other sets at the Book 1 or 2 level on his own.

In some reading schemes, especially in the early books, the text is arranged so that the line breaks emphasize the grouping of words into meaningful units which in itself helps him to understand what he is reading, even when the teacher is not there.

A simple system of grading books (eg by sticking a square of coloured paper on them, green for the simplest, blue for the next level of difficulty, red for the next, and so on) allows the teacher to put books in the library corner for a child to choose for himself, within the limits of his reading ability. He may sometimes choose to look at a book from a more difficult section than the one he normally uses, but if he does so, he does it in the knowledge that he will find the text difficult. But it is important to encourage him to read within his ability, not only to consolidate simple reading skills and to develop others, but so that he may find reading rewarding and enjoyable.

The teacher can sometimes discuss the stories with the children, asking them about the different characters, and giving them an opportunity to re-tell the stories to other children. Acting is always a useful setting for discussing a story. 'How do you think such-and-such a character would speak? How did the Queen feel when the mirror said that Snow White was prettier than she was?' become practical questions when the story is being acted and the children are portraying the characters.

Playing with miniature characters from books (such as 'Story People') or acting a story they have heard *before* they read the text, helps reading skills to grow out of the children's experience of play; acting a story *after* it has been read is a new stage, but the link between the imaginary worlds of play and those built up through language is still strong.

A dramatic reading of even a simple story from the basic reading scheme being used can have this kind of advantage. The children have already read the book. They know the words and are accustomed to the sentences. To re-read the text in a new and interesting way gives further straightforward practice, as well as opening up opportunities for discussion and interpretation.

Reading stories to the children continues to be important for the development of their own reading skills, so that the teacher should learn to read as well as she can herself, and be prepared to use tapes and records to give the children experience of other voices and interpretations of the written word.

Stories which the children can later read for themselves should be included. *Beacon Readers* contain many folk-tales well told in simple language, which an adult reading can make evocative and exciting; some of the stories in *Nippers* are useful, using a more realistic background and ordinary children; Mollie Clarke's *First Folk Tales* and *Second Folk Tales* include stories from many other countries, so that the children not only learn about other people and the way they look at life through listening to the folk stories and looking at the pictures, but also immigrant children may find in some of the books a background which is familiar and a story which they already know and can share with other children. These are just a few examples; there are many other such books, and more are being published all the time.

If the story is one which the children can read for themselves, the teacher may sometimes begin reading it aloud, and then leave it at an exciting point for the children to finish on their own. There are three advantages in this: the children are encouraged to read, and learn to read by reading; the teacher uses all her skills in reading aloud to give full meaning and colour to the words, thus building up the scene and characters in the children's minds; and because their attention can be given at first entirely to listening and thinking, the whole scene for the story is already there in their imagination when they come to read the rest of the text for themselves, and so the words carry a richer meaning.

But there are skills which children should develop other than reading straight through a text and using their imagination and experience to give it life, though this is important even where factual material is being read.

Different ways of reading are appropriate with different materials: if a poem is being read silently, it is helpful to be able to hear the words internally, to give full value to their sound; if one is reading a recipe, a swift skimming of the text, picking out important words, may be more appropriate.

Children have to learn how to find information; how to use a dictionary; how to read in order to answer specific questions; how to use a table of contents; how words are arranged alphabetically in an index; how to skim through a book looking for the headings and information they need. They have to learn how to read a passage and pick out the important facts or ideas; how to check statements made in a book against other sources of information. Later, as they grow older, they have to learn how a biased presentation can be recognized, and what is meant by the emotive use of words.

This kind of learning should develop and continue throughout their school lives, but a beginning can be made even in the early stages of reading. The teaching need not be formal; it is often best done as part of other activities which are going on in the classroom and through subjects other than reading, or even 'English' at the secondary school stage. In making and using a picture dictionary, children encounter the need to arrange words alphabetically. The knowledge acquired in this way might soon be used in looking up the name of a bird seen for the first time, or information about the feeding and habits of a new pet. Having to find out facts connected with some project, and reporting back to the class, provides a useful opportunity for learning how to look things up in a book, pick out important facts, and record them. There may sometimes be specific as well as incidental teaching. When a group of children need this information, then the group might be taught together. In learning a new skill teaching is more effective if the learner sees the purpose of what he is doing (because then he brings his energies and attention to bear on it) and the new knowledge is more likely to be retained if it is quickly put to use.

This does not mean that the teacher sits back and waits for such opportunities to arise: she is alert to use those which occur, but she also creates them. She might, for example, arrange with a teacher in another area an exchange of letters between the children in the two schools, an exchange which could include pictures of the area in which the children lived, and accounts of what the people do. With older children, this might include a study of local newspapers. Or she might introduce a bird-table, or gerbils as new pets, just at the point when the children were ready to look up information. Making puppets provides an opportunity for learning to follow simple instructions; so does a recipe in cooking. Specific lessons in finding the answers to a given set of questions, using information books, fit into place when the children see the purpose of what they are doing.

Many experienced teachers encourage the children to question what they read very early, and such questioning can apply to fiction as well as to reading for information. Over the years, I have had many letters from children who are learning to read using books I have written. Sometimes they question the pictures: '... in Book 9 of the *Griffin Pirate Stories* there is a mistake on Page 25. The mistake is that you don't play a flute like that, you put it sideways against your mouth.' (Fortunately for the author, some of the most ancient flutes were played like recorders.) Sometimes the children show special knowledge, like a boy from the Isles of Scilly who wrote: 'On Page 28 of *The Ice King's Daughter*,* Druan has left his oars in the rowlocks. Nobody who has a punt would leave them in because they might slip out. You pull the oars in-board.' Since the only reply possible to this is to thank the writer and promise to try to avoid such mistakes in the future, the children learn that adults are not infallible. This is the kind of critical reading, checking the words against the pictures and against experience, which can be developed from the beginning and certainly in the junior school. The examples quoted also show how experienced teachers seize an opportunity for purposeful letter writing.

Any text should be checked against the children's own knowledge and experience. If they are in any doubt, the facts can be looked up. If the teacher has reference books available and uses them when a child asks a question to which she does not know the answer, then the children learn how to find out. They also learn that finding out, rather than covering up, is the appropriate response to lack of knowledge. If any child has special information, he should be encouraged to contribute it, while books of reference should be available as soon as they can be read well enough.

Sometimes the letters I receive show that the author has left loose ends in the story. For example, one letter reads: I have been reading *The Three Witches** and I want to know what happened to the Red Witch's cat and the Black Witch's cat when the witches were blown away please can you tell me.' This kind of question in class provides the teacher with the opportunity of saying: What do *you* think happened? The children can tell, write or illustrate the answer to that question, according to their age and ability in writing. (A similar situation can be created if the teacher deliberately makes up the first part of a story, and then leaves it in the air.) But in my experience, children may still want to know 'What *really* happened?' and will only be satisfied by an answer from the writer of the story. It is as if the imaginary world is so real to children, that there can be only one answer to the question, an account of an event which actually occurred in the secondary world of the story.

* *Dragon Pirate Stories*

Interpreting the writer's meaning

The point has already been made* that whereas a child's own book is a record of his own ideas, when he reads a published book he has to interpret someone else's words through his own experience and imagination. There is a further stage in learning to read which is of equal importance. We have to learn to understand, to the best of our ability, what the *writer* means by the words he has used, rather than simply interpreting those words in our own terms.

For each of us, our background and experience of life is unique. No two people bring precisely the same experiences to bear on the meaning of any word. As Ronald Morris says, 'Your dog is not my dog.... Words have a life of their own in the mind of the individual. We dress our concepts in the clothing available to us from the wardrobe of our own experience.'† This means that when we read a story, an argument, or indeed any piece of prose, we see it through the glass of our individual lives. This is, of course, equally true when we listen to spoken words. Sometimes the glass is a distorting one. To give a simple example, I remember as a child of eight being severely reprimanded by my teacher for saying 'Dash!' when I broke my pencil. I can still remember my feeling of incomprehension at the reason for the rebuke. To me, 'dash' meant no more than 'bother', a simple exclamation. To her (it was a long time ago, and she was elderly then) it meant a line in a text standing for some unmentionable word.

It is yet another stage in learning to read, to realize that in order to understand a text, we have to give the author's value to the words he uses, rather than our own. We may, at the same time, use our experience in considering critically what he has to say. But in order to understand first what that is, we must do our best to realize what the words mean to him, and here again we have to imagine ourselves as well as we can into another person's life, looking out on the world through his eyes. The importance of reading and listening to stories in order to understand other people and ourselves has already been stressed. We need now to extend this kind of understanding to the writer of the text, as well as the characters he depicts.

* See p 43
† What Childuren Learn in Learning to Read in *English in Education*, vol 5 No 3.

To be able to do this, is to read at a very mature level. It means interpreting individual words within the context of the whole. It also means using any knowledge one may have of the author's background, his experiences and the place and time at which he lived, in order to recognize that some words may have a different meaning from that which they carry for us. When Robert Frost writes of a 'yellow wood', all the brilliant colour of the woods in the New England fall lies behind his words; an Englishman reading them with only the experience of English woods in autumn has to make a special effort of imagination to give the words their full value. Someone from the tropics would have to make a still greater effort of understanding. When the older version of the prayer-book speaks of people who 'indifferently administer justice', we have consciously to interpret 'indifferently' as 'impartially' before we know what is meant. English is used all over the world, and the same word can have very different meanings in different countries, as any Englishman who is foolish enough to call a Canadian an ass rapidly discovers; so does the American child who tells his English hostess that there are bugs in his bedroom.

Because of their inevitably limited experience, children can often totally misinterpret words, and it is only through discussion or illustration that we and they can become aware of this. The story of the small boy who illustrated 'the flight into Egypt' by a picture of the Holy Family boarding an aeroplane, with Pontius as the pilot, is almost certainly apocryphal, but I once read *Flannen Isle* with a group of intelligent twelve-year-olds, many of whom visualized 'a half-tide reef' as an incomplete reef-knot.

But all these are relatively obvious examples. There are for all of us much slighter variations in meanings and emphasis which are all the more dangerous for being so small that they can normally be ignored. To become aware of this problem of communication is to take another step forward in learning to read, a step which some readers never take at all.

It may be thought that such a mature level of reading is a matter for the university and adult education, rather than the school. It is true that we continue to learn how to read throughout our lives, and the teachers of older children and students are still teachers of reading. But children can be helped to become aware of the idea underlying this principle quite early. I remember seeing Humbert Wolfe's poem about a blackbird in an American child's reader. It was illustrated, and the picture showed a red-winged blackbird, the only one an American child would associate with the poem. Such an illustration provides an opportunity for explaining that 'My dog is not your dog'. One can take a simple word, such as 'cat', and ask the children to shut their eyes and picture the animal. If they then describe, or draw, the picture they have seen, they soon realize that each one of them has a different cat. In the same way, characters in a story may be pictured, and with older children the differences can be discussed, and also the type of character the *author* had in mind can be considered, and how far the text supports their own ideas. Film versions of books are another useful source of materials for discussions and comparisons. Letters in local newspapers and replies to such letters sometimes provide material showing how variously different people interpret happenings, words, descriptions and arguments.

The way in which children are taught to read is important for their later reading. As teachers, we need to use opportunities for teaching skills and developing attitudes in the earlier stages of learning, so that in the end 'we can hope to achieve a more mature level where the reader can maintain a balance between responding freely as a person to the message of the text as he first reads it and reaching out more critically in his search for the exact intention of the author'.*

Children's writing

It will have been clear from the beginning how much speaking, reading and writing are all part of learning to read. 'Reading maketh a full man; conference a ready man; writing an exact man' is still good advice. We learn to study words, to think about their meaning, in using them ourselves.

In the beginning, writing down a sentence means paying close attention to the letters, to the structure of the words. Later, in writing even a brief account, the meaning of the words used must be carefully considered and a child giving a report on some special event or interest may need to look up, and perhaps explain to others, the meaning of simple technical terms. In writing their own poetry, the children's attention is drawn to the sounds and meanings of words and to the associations and feelings they evoke, as an essential part

* Ronald Morris: *What Children Learn in Learning to Read*

of the writing. The knowledge and experience they gain enriches their later reading.

In writing as in reading, if attention is concentrated on the sheer mechanics of the skill—the formation of letters, spelling and punctuation, grammar—then the mind is not free to think about the content of what is being written. The flow of ideas is held in check. This does not mean that these mechanical skills are unimportant; it does mean that they have sometimes to be attended to separately. For example, children in infant schools can often make up stories which they will tell, and which sometimes fascinate other children. If these are to be recorded, the teacher has to write them down or use a tape-recorder. The effort of writing them themselves would so absorb the children's attention, and take up so much time and effort, that little or nothing would be left for the flow of ideas. As the children grow more competent in writing, they can be asked to write original material, but if it requires much thought and imagination, at least the first draft should be written in such a way that the problem of concentration on the act of writing words is reduced to a minimum: in pencil, for example and without worrying *in the first instance* too much about spelling and punctuation. Even an adult, writing an important letter or some other piece of difficult prose, makes a rough draft. The time to make sure that the writing is clear and the spelling correct is when the finished work has to be read by other people—if the child's story is to be 'published' as a book to put in the class library, or a notice is to be put up on the board, or a letter written to someone else.

If a child makes an anthology of poems he likes, his actual writing may, in one part of the activity, have his almost undivided attention. There will also be other occasions when less original thinking is being demanded, and then more emphasis can be laid on correct spelling and punctuation and clear writing. Again, specific lessons can be given to meet specific needs, for example in teaching the children how to spell a group of words they need, or spell incorrectly. When a child has written something which is going to be read by other people, the perfect opportunity arises for the teacher to go through it with him to 'get it right'. In an interview reported in the *Times Educational Supplement,** Charles Causely

* *Times Educational Supplement* 17.11.72. *Haiku in The Park*, Norman Hidden talks to Charles Causley

mentioned that his class (in a junior school) had produced two books of poems which had been published. (Every child in the class contributed at least one poem.) He added, 'I think if it's going into print, the spelling should be correct. I saw a selection recently ... in which the little boy wrote about sausages and the teacher left it spelt *sossijes*. This is an adult jest, no sensible teacher would ever print a wrong form, it's humiliating for the child.'

This is surely a very important point. When others are going to read a child's book (and this means other children, teachers in the school, or parents, as well as times when it is read by a wider group of adults and older children) then the child and the teacher work together to present it correctly. The teacher is working on the child's side, and any corrections of sentences or spelling are not criticisms of the child and his way of expressing himself: they are supportive, *avoiding* humiliation of any kind for him; avoiding, too, the adult jest. They mean taking the child's work seriously. Specific systematic teaching of writing and spelling has its place, and children accept this, when they see its purpose and when their newly acquired skills are being put to good use. Apparently meaningless practice should be avoided because it is ineffective and stultifying. If a child has accepted that a skill is important to him, he will tolerate a great deal of practice in order to improve, especially if he is aware of increasing proficiency and success.

This book is concerned with the teaching of reading, so that related skills are mentioned only briefly. They are closely connected with learning to read, but it is always important to remember that there should be times when children are free to read books of their own choice, without being expected to answer questions or to discuss contents, or to make any overt response. The most powerful incentive in learning to read is the reward which comes from mastering the content of the books themselves and there should always be time for books to make their own impact without hinderance or interference, no matter how well meant and planned this may be.

NOTES ON BOOKS FOR FURTHER READING

It is not enough to read texts about the teaching of reading, if we as teachers and parents want children to become aware of the excitement, the extension of experience, the new worlds to be found through reading. We need to know the books themselves. Fortunately really good books for children are more than just 'children's books': they have something to offer an adult reader too. But few teachers have time to read many of the books being written for children today, and unless they make an effort to keep in touch with what is being published, they may rely too heavily on children's classics of past generations in choosing books to read to their classes.

Children's Literature in Education founded by Sidney Robbins is an exceptionally interesting periodical, full of stimulating ideas and a source of invaluable information about writers. Reading it will help books to come alive for the teacher and, through her, for the children.

A Sense of Story, by John Rowe Townsend contains a series of essays on nineteen leading English-language writers, who are writing for children today. There is a brief biography, followed by a critical survey of the work of each writer and a list of his or her books. *The Nesbit Tradition: The Children's Novel 1945–1970* by Marcus Crouch is another interesting critical survey and *Intent upon Reading*, by Margery Fisher, is an enlightening book about stories for children. *Matters of fact: aspects of non-fiction for children* by the same writer is equally helpful.

Wallace Hildick's book *Children and Fiction* has already been mentioned, because of the chapter on 'readers'. This is the only book I know in which the writer seriously considers the effects of methods of learning to read on children's later interest in literature, and even here it is only briefly considered. But this is a valuable book for teachers of reading for the same reason that *A Sense of Story* is valuable: it considers children's books seriously and critically, as literature. It accepts that books provide imaginative experience, and is concerned with the quality of that experience.

There is another group of books from which adults can gain insight and understanding of children: autobiographical novels, autobiographies, and stories about children written for adults. If we accept that, through reading, we can widen our experience imaginatively and learn to look at the world through another person's eyes, then we should not neglect the opportunities for increasing understanding which come from reading books in which some of the characters are children. In creating his characters, the writer inevitably calls on his own experiences as a child, and his own observations and insights as an adult. These can be illuminating. If you want to discover what it was like to be an aviator in the early days of flying, you are likely to learn something from Saint-Exupéry's *Wind, Sand and Stars* which you cannot learn from a history of aviation. In the same way, it is possible to learn something about children and learning to read from books other than educational texts. There are many such books. The two following short stories illustrate the kind of reading which provides such experience.

Les Bottes de Sept Lieves (The Seven-League Boots) by Marcel Aymé is a story through which a reader can re-enter and experience from the inside, as it were, the imaginative world of young children. It is to be found in French and in translation in *French Short Stories* (Penguin Parallel Texts) published by Penguin Books.

Baa Baa, Black Sheep (to be found in *Wee Willie Winkie*, by Rudyard Kipling) includes an account of a boy learning to read. It is a story of a boy who finds himself labelled as a black sheep. The milieu is dated; there is a touch of snobbery to be discounted; but it is well worth reading for the insight it gives into the child's feelings and the way he responds to the adults around him.

8

The help which parents can give

Many parents would like to help their children specifically with their learning. Such help is most effective when there is close co-operation between home and school, when the teachers take time to explain to the parents the underlying reasons for what goes on in school, and the parents take an interest in what is happening. Both sides have a great deal to learn from each other about the child: the teacher sees him professionally and the parents have unrivalled knowledge of his growth and experiences to date. This chapter is principally for parents who, realizing the importance of literacy in its widest sense, want to help their children learn to read.

There will never be real equality of opportunity for all children in education, because of the important part played by other human beings in their learning. Even if all our school buildings, equipment and the courses offered by the schools were the same, perfect equality of opportunity would still not exist, because children come to school from different homes, with different needs and abilities. Some teachers will always be more efficient than others, and the same teacher may not be equally effective with different children, but even if all the teachers were perfect, complete equality could not exist because of the vital importance of the children's parents and homes in their lives and development. The warm, supportive home gives a child confidence in learning and in making new relationships when he comes to school. A stimulating home environment encourages him to investigate and learn.

This is an immense subject and in this chapter only one aspect of it can be briefly considered: how can parents help their children learn to read? Although the main responsibility for teaching reading falls on the schools, the parents' help and support can be invaluable.

a BEFORE A CHILD GOES TO SCHOOL

The foundations of a child's later learning are laid during the first years of his life, before he enters any school. During this time he learns to respond to other people, to look and to listen, to explore the world around him. One of the most important tools in this exploration and learning is language, and during the first five years of his life the normal child learns to communicate through speech. (Even if the language spoken in his home is different from that which he will later use in school, he learns what language is, to listen, to respond, and to use spoken words.) For a normal child speech comes before reading, and he gradually builds up one vocabulary of words which he uses himself and one of words which he understands when he hears other people use them. We all have several vocabularies of varying size: the number of words which we understand is likely to be greater than the number we use ourselves in speaking. Even when we are adults the number of words in our reading vocabulary is likely to be greater than that in our writing vocabulary.

Children learn to speak through listening to someone talking to them. The importance of parents talking to their young children is being emphasized more and more because it helps to develop 'oracy'—the term used in relation to spoken language with roughly the same meaning as literacy in relation to written and printed language. Oracy is the foundation of literacy. The talking does not have to be arranged as a set piece; all that is necessary is that a parent should talk to a young child in the ordinary course of living, commenting on what is going on, naming objects, describing things. There is no special vocabulary which should be used, and although sentences should not be too long or involved, and the ideas expressed should be those a child is likely to understand, there should be no talking down to the children. Many parents do all this naturally and without consciously thinking about it: a mother who talks to her baby as she baths him, or as he plays on the floor while she is doing the household chores, is helping him to learn to speak and laying the foundation for learning to read. A father who lets his small son or daughter help him in the garden, or in mending something about the house, or the mother who lets the child cook something when she is cooking, is building up the child's vocabulary and experience in a most valuable way.

There are special times when more direct help can be given: when parents read stories to their children, and look at the pictures in picture-books with them, asking them to name or count objects, pointing out colours or naming new things, discussing what they see and what is happening in the picture.

Parents have a great advantage here. They are in a one-to-one relationship with the child, and can give him their undivided attention for an extended period of time, something rarely possible for the busy teacher. Those who find it difficult to frame questions might use a series such as Macdonald's *Zero Books*, which are primarily picture books, but which have a number of suggested questions for parents to ask about each picture at the bottom of the page. But any picture book, or any picture, can serve as a starting point for a discussion, for naming things and asking questions.

As soon as the child begins to speak himself, it would perhaps be better to say that parents can help by talking *with* their children, rather than by talking *to* them, for it is important to listen too. Some adults are better talkers than listeners, and children need both.

The way in which a child learns a new word has already been described: the new word names an experience. Parents can help children to build up a wide vocabulary by giving them opportunities for experience, and then using words to describe the experience for them, in the same way that a teacher does in a nursery or infant school. 'Look at that cat. What a big cat he is! Let's stroke him,' is a very simple example of everyday learning of this kind. A more deliberately contrived experience could be provided by a bag of different odds and ends of cloth and materials which a child might look through, feeling the ones which are soft, the ones which are hard, the ones which are scratchy; or naming the coloured pieces, red, blue, yellow, green, black. Helping a child to put away toys, and taking the time to say: 'Put this one on the bottom shelf', 'This one goes in that box', 'This one goes under the table', 'The teddy sits on top of the box', 'Let's put the big doll up here. Where shall we put the little dog?' is important in teaching the meaning of words. The sentences should not be forced. They should simply be part of the activity, their meaning being made clear by the actions which accompany them and the whole context in which they are used.

The importance of giving children opportunities for imaginative play cannot be overstressed. The link between the imaginary worlds built up by children using toys (or sticks and stones), and their later reading, when the imaginary world is created through words, has already been indicated. It is not easy to allow children opportunities for all the free play they need in a small house, especially if there is no garden, but a reasonable amount of space should be set aside for it, and a reasonable amount of mess tolerated, at least for limited periods. A child whose home is kept so clean and tidy that he can never paint or draw or build or scatter his toys around may be suffering a real deprivation. If there is a garden, it is so often a neatly kept and cared for parental reserve, not considered as a place where a small child could play and gain experience. Of course parents have their rights too, but if space can be spared for a pile of sand (covered to guard it from cats) and there are bushes where a child can hide, this provides a background in which imagination can develop as he grows older. A corner of the yard shut off by a hurdle or a low wall, or the simplest play-house built of boards, becomes a place where a child can be alone or play with his friends. It can be a house, a castle, a cave or a robber's den in imaginative play. Many homes have no space for such things, but in houses where there are gardens or backyards a little planning may provide not only opportunities for play, but also allow the adults more peace and quiet while young children are absorbed in their own imaginings.

Young children need toys which encourage them to use their imagination, including simple dressing up clothes, dolls and other small figures to play with when creating imaginary worlds. The dressing up clothes need not be elaborate: one can only be a Red Indian in a Red Indian's outfit, but a red cloak will grace a king or Red Riding Hood, a robber or a grandmother. The little figures need not necessarily be bought. Very simple ones can be made from odd materials, for example with wooden beads for heads and bodies made from cylinders of thin rolled cardboard, with pipe-cleaners for arms. Painting their faces and clothes becomes part of the child's imaginative play, as he turns them into different characters. The wooden Story People* of the reading scheme *One, Two, Three and Away!* make a direct link between this kind of fantasy play and books, but even without such a direct connection, the very creation of a number of 'worlds', using toys, is part of the background experience of learning to read. The imaginary world the child makes is not the one of the dolls and houses set out on the floor, but the one he builds up in his own mind, using the toys as concrete symbols. As he grows older, these will be replaced by other symbols: words.

* See page 45 and the photographs on plates IV and V

Imagination is encouraged by other toys which have general rather than specific uses: bricks which can be built into houses or castles, aeroplanes, ships and all kinds of imaginary buildings may be more stimulating for young children than a set which has to be built into a house and nothing else.

As the children grow older, too, expeditions of all kinds become a fruitful source of new experiences: going to the shops, a walk in a park or down to the bus station, a trip to the seaside, a visit to a zoo. The new experiences lead to new learning, and to an extension of vocabulary as the adults talk with the children about what they see and do.

Reading or telling stories to children is a vitally important part of this background. If parents do not want to read the stories themselves, they can let the children listen to those on the radio or, if they have the necessary equipment, to the many records and tape-recordings which are available. Public libraries sometimes organize story times for children. But those parents who do read stories to and with their children are providing a wealth of imaginative material for them and teaching them implicitly that books are rewarding and that reading is a door into new worlds. Rhymes and verses and poetry all add richness to experience and draw attention, without the matter even being mentioned, to the sounds of words. To listen to a story or poem read by an adult, to talk about it and ask questions while sitting perhaps on his father's or mother's knee and enjoying the warmth of physical contact, is a different experience to that of simply listening to a recording (though less will be lost if parents and children listen to records or radio stories together).

Seeing a story on television does not replace the experience of listening to one. Watching television may help to increase a child's vocabulary in some ways, though too much passive watching might mean that he had too little time for first-hand experience. But in any case the story seen on the screen is imagined *for* the child, and this can be a limiting, as well as an enriching experience. (It can also be a more horrifying and frightening experience, if clothed in all the realities of visual presentation. 'Three Blind Mice' may be acceptable as a nursery rhyme, but it would carry a different meaning seen in realistic detail on a screen.)

In listening to a story, as later in reading one, the child uses all the experiences he has had to set the stage and people it with characters. The illustrations in books often help (especially if the background to the story is a strange one) if the pictures are seen when the story is first heard or told and if they interpret the words used in the telling.

As the stories are read, the children learn what books are and the value of being able to read. But stories which are told have a value all their own, too, because it is often easier to *tell* a story well, with the dramatic emphasis and gestures which make it live, than it is to read it. The teller looks at the child and not at the book, and so holds his attention.

Being encouraged and expected to do some things for themselves helps children to be ready to undertake simple tasks. A flexible routine helps them to learn to settle down, to find a reassuring order in their existence. Both these experiences are important when they go to school. But perhaps the most important matter which children learn in the home is the reassurance which comes from being loved and cared for, so that they are not afraid of new relationships, of exploring and finding out about the world around them.

There are other experiences which help a child to learn when he goes to school. Being asked to help adults and carry out simple routines like putting away toys, all help him to learn to co-operate. So do contacts with other children, whether they are siblings, the children of friends and neighbours, or children he meets in a play group or nursery school. Whether a child should join a specially organized group is a matter for the parents to decide, and some children need and respond to such a group more than others. It is a great help to many children when they reach school to have experienced free play in an ordered community, where the very fact that there are other children means learning to take turns, to listen, to share things, to respond to a simple request, to be for a short period without their parents.

In all this, there is no specific teaching of reading. If a child shows an interest in words—for example, the caption of a picture, his own name, words he sees written up about him —then the adult helps him by responding and reading the words to him. As in teaching, the child's interest and response are a good indication of how far one should go. There is no sudden change in a child at five years of age, and some of the activities suggested for a child of school age might be useful with a younger one who was very interested in reading. But going to school marks a big step in a child's life, and parents can help to prepare him for it.

b WHEN A CHILD GOES TO SCHOOL

Here again, the parents' role is immensely important, but it is mainly a supportive one. Going to school is a major step in a child's life. He leaves his home and familiar surroundings for the first time, and finds himself in a world where he is among many other children of the same age and where he must share an adult with a large group.

From the child's point of view, it may be a time of some anxiety. If there are younger children, he has to leave them behind in full possession of the home and probably of his mother while he is away, and he may need and perhaps demand special attention when he gets back from school. It is a time, too, when adults compare him with others of his own age, and he becomes aware of his own abilities and development in relation to that of other children. It is wise to remember that there are wide normal variations in the way children develop, and to be chary of comparisons. It can and should be an immensely interesting time for the child. It is a period of discovery, of learning to stand on his own feet; but it is also a time when he needs his parents' as well as his teacher's support and encouragement.

Continuing to read stories to children, to look at and discuss pictures, and to talk with them about things which are happening and which interest the children, is still an important part of the background of reading, but some parents want to do more than this, especially if a child seems to be having difficulties in learning. They want to help with specific teaching. Some parents can and do help to teach their children to read, but there are a number of problems to be considered.

The first is that of the emotions likely to be aroused by such teaching. The analogy of learning to drive a car has already been used, and it is sometimes said that husbands and wives should never teach each other to drive. The fact that the spouse is unlikely to be a skilled teacher is only part of the difficulty. The real problem is that the emotional tie between them is so strong that the mistakes, which are an inevitable part of learning, matter too much. The learner wants to do well, to stand well in the eyes of the teacher, and too many other complicated feelings and emotions enter into the learning situation. Some people can cope happily with the situation; others cannot. Similarly, if a child is being taught by a parent, the emotions aroused by mistakes or failures may be very strong. The parent, unused to teaching other chidren of the same age, may also feel that the child is being stupid, or slow, or not working hard enough. Mistakes matter far too much. Over-anxiety on the part of a parent can be communicated to the child; it also puts a weapon into the hands of a child who wants a device for getting his parents' attention. If a parent is teaching a child anything to do with reading, if he is simply hearing him read from a work he knows well, there is a golden rule to be followed: such help should only be given if both the child and the parent are enjoying themselves. If either side becomes anxious or unhappy, it is wise to stop.

The second problem is one of method. Teaching is a skilled occupation and ways of teaching have changed. A conflict of methods between home and school may confuse the child. This problem can of course be overcome if the parent works closely with the teacher, and the teacher arranges specific activities (including reading a book or a page the child can already read) to be done at home. When a child brings his work home there is another golden rule here for both parents and teachers: never laugh at or disparage a child's efforts, at the models he has made, the pictures he has painted, the books he has written and illustrated, unless he intended them to be funny. Accept them as he does, encourage him to say as much as he wants to about them but do not press him, and avoid adult jokes and anecdotes over his head. Nothing takes away a child's confidence and interest more quickly than for him to create something in all seriousness (and everything we create is in some sense part of ourselves), to take it home with pride, only to have adults find it silly, or a matter for jest among themselves.

But if parents really want to help their children specifically to learn to read there is one group of materials which can be extremely useful: reading games. Sometimes these are part of a reading scheme, but home-made games can be effective too. If the parents play a reading game *as a game* with the children at home, as something the children choose to play and which everyone enjoys, useful practice in reading may be provided without the problems already mentioned arising. It is not difficult for parents to devise matching and quest games using words from the readers the child uses in school or other words he sees frequently.

Reading *with* children can be developed alongside reading *to* them. Children who frequently hear short stories often come to know them virtually by heart, and sometimes to take a child on one's knee, and read the story to him, running a finger along under the print while one reads, is one way of showing him that printed marks stand for spoken words, and that reading goes from left to right. There are many richly illustrated children's books with simple texts through which printed words and sentences can be introduced to young children. If parents simply point to a caption under a picture, and add: 'Look. This says ...' they are helping the child to see and recognize words, without any formal teaching. The important point is again that everyone should enjoy the experience.

Macdonald's *Zero Books* have already been mentioned as picture books, and there is a whole series of *Picture Puffins*; Macdonald *Starters* are for children who are beginning to learn to read. There is a series of books originating in New Zealand, by Jane Melser, also published in this country, in which parents would find stimulating ideas for helping children to develop spoken language. The titles alone are suggestive: *What is little? What is big? What goes fast? What comes down? What can jump? What goes up? What goes round and round?* Methuen's *Number-Story Caption Books* provide many opportunities for extending vocabulary, and again the titles alone indicate the kind of language experience they stimulate: *Huge and Tiny, Too Large and Too Small, Over and Under.* In fact, there is a wealth of books from many publishers which are sold simply as children's books, which help parents and teachers to provide a rich background of experience for children who are just beginning school, and which sometimes provide more nourishment for their imagination than the inevitably rather limited texts of their first readers.

*Stories to Start With** is a series designed as a link between stories to be read *to* children and the very first books they read for themselves. There is a book of 'long' stories for the adult to read aloud, and accompanying books in which each story is re-told in pictures with very simple captions for the child. In using these books, a parent first reads the longer story to the child, and then they both look at the short story in the child's book together, discussing the pictures and discovering what the captions 'say'. It should not be long before most children begin to recognize or remember many of the words, although they might not know them out of context; but the purpose of the books is to help them to understand what reading is, rather than to build up a basic sight vocabulary.

* Sheila McCullagh

There is a further important factor to be considered, and that is the one of the more general attitudes in the home. In his study of *Educational Opportunity and the Home*, Dr Miller found that 'children who gain most educational opportunity tend strongly to come from homes where independent thinking and freedom of discussion among all members is the rule'. In such homes the children are not over-indulged, but their 'curiosity and academic aspirations are supported and encouraged by the parents'. On the other hand, children who were least able to profit from educational opportunities came from homes where 'their thought is dominated by parents, and the children themselves accept this as reasonable'. Although this was only part of a 'climate of general deprivation, with elements of social, cultural, intellectual and emotional deprivation', Dr Miller found that these factors, 'while more likely to be found in working class families, are also prevalent in some middle class families to a greater extent than … is popularly thought'. So that it is not only *what* is provided for the children, but the *way* in which it is provided, which matters, and the fundamental importance of attitudes towards learning (in every sense of the word) is again underlined. What is said here in relation to education generally is equally applicable to reading. Creating a climate in the home which encourages learning is certainly at least as important as creating a climate of literacy in school.

It is through the creation of this kind of background that parents can help children who are learning to read. The advantages of close co-operation between home and school are clear. If there is no conflict of purpose between the two, and if the school explains how the children are being educated and taught to read, the parents not only understand where they can help, but parental anxiety is avoided. Parents and teachers can work together in helping children acquire the fundamental skill which encourages further independent learning: the skill of reading.

Appendix

Appendix

Appendix

(a) *The language-experience approach* and *Breakthrough to Literacy*

The language-experience approach to the teaching of reading will be a familiar one to many teachers, although they do not necessarily call it by that name. It simply means basing the children's first reading materials on things which have happened to them. The experience is discussed by the teacher with a group of children, and the teacher records the children's comments, usually on a blackboard. These are then discussed, rearranged in order, and again recorded by the teacher and sometimes by the group or by individual children. The children usually provide the illustrations. Sometimes a large class-book is made, sometimes the method is adapted to individual work, in which the children make their own books.

It will be seen that the basic idea underlying the language-experience approach is that of providing first books and reading material which is written in language the children understand because it is their own, and which is rich in meaning because it refers to direct experience which they have had. It will be clear that such an approach can be formal or informal. Its strength is that the material is related to the background of the group and even of individual children, in a way in which no published material can be. Its drawbacks are that it makes heavy demands on the teacher if it is to be effective (and especially, of course, if it is the only approach being used) and that it may provide the children with a basic sight vocabulary comprised of words relating only to their immediate environment. If the books which follow are to be about anything else (if they are to include fairy-tales, for example), so many new words have to be introduced to build up new imaginary worlds that the gradation of difficulty is steep and the temptation is to confine all the stories to the everyday environment of the children.

Breakthrough to Literacy is included here because it also is a scheme which seeks to make early reading relevant to the children by using their own language in the early stages. It encourages them to make their own reading materials by providing separate printed words which can be fitted into 'sentence makers'. (There are blanks, too, on which any new word a child wants can be printed, so that no one predetermines what vocabulary the children use.) The advantage of such materials is that they enable the children to make up their own printed sentences from the beginning, but relieve them of the burden of writing the words. To quote the handbook: 'The Sentence Maker is the heart of the literary work. In using this piece of equipment the responsibility for ordering written English for the first time falls upon the child, and at the same time he is composing his first reading book.'

As the quotation indicates, *Breakthrough to Literacy* also stresses the linguistic approach: in the course of their work, the children will discover many important facts about printed language, eg the left to right direction of reading, the meaning of the terms 'word' and 'sentence' and the way in which sentences are made up of separate words. These are all points which cannot be taken for granted, and *Breakthrough to Literacy* helps a child to learn about language by actually handling it.

As those who have read Sylvia Ashton-Warner's *Teacher* will know, books the children make for themselves can be a good deal less conventional and limited than many published readers. They can also be just as limited. It all depends on the teacher. It is clear, too, that it is possible to use this approach in conjunction with other published reading schemes, and this is already the practice of many teachers.

(b) *i.t.a., Words in Colour* and *Colour Story Reading*

It has long been recognized that one of the difficulties in learning to read and write English is the fact that the same sound may be represented by several different letters and letter-combinations. In other words, there is no one-to-one phoneme/grapheme relationship.

Attempts to achieve such a relationship, or as near an approximation to it as possible, are not new, but over the last decade experimental work has been carried out on a more widespread scale than ever before.

The solution presented by i.t.a. is to increase the number of graphemes (ie letters or symbols) in the alphabet, until there are enough to represent virtually all phonemes (ie sounds).

It is claimed that, because the printed words are recorded consistently, children come to understand the alphabetic principle quickly, and are encouraged to work independently. They are not put off by variations which seem to them illogical or inexplicable. Many teachers using i.t.a. think that the children are also free to write their ideas down much more readily, because the children feel that they have a medium which they can use themselves without making mistakes.

Results of experiments in teaching reading have to be regarded with caution, because there is evidence to suggest that any reading drive on the part of teachers will increase the children's levels of competence in reading, no matter what the method, and because the final evaluation can only be made after the children have transferred to books printed in traditional orthography. The fact that children learning to read in a special media are to some extent debarred from reading widely in books outside the particular reading scheme has also to be taken into consideration, though if the medium were more generally adopted this objection would have less force. After a very thorough investigation, Warburton and Southgate came to the conclusion that 'i.t.a. is a superior medium to t.o. in teaching young children to read', but that 'this advantage may be lost after the transition'. They suggest that further research is 'highly desirable'.

In *Words in Colour*, Gattegno uses a system of colours to achieve phonic regularity. He uses 41 colours (where i.t.a. uses 44 characters) to regularize phoneme/grapheme relationships. The teaching suggested is, to begin with, very much a matter of training the children to make a given sound when shown a particular colour, and to respond to a repeated letter by repeating the sound, indicating the duration in time of words according to the lengths of groups of letters. It provides a structural approach, based on group or class teaching, which is much more formal than that usually found in most schools.

The comment of Joan Dean, in her paper on *Words in Colour* published in *The Second International Reading Symposium*, on the books which accompany the scheme is relevant: 'The purpose of these [books] is to provide reading material which gives practice with words which contain all the possible spellings of all the sounds of English. As you will appreciate, it is difficult to combine this with reading material which is within the children's understanding and which is of real interest to them in terms of meaning.'

Colour Story Reading sets out to use four colours to indicate *phonic rules*, as well as particular sounds. For example, all long vowels are printed in red, and blue circles indicate silent letters. Nine background shapes always stand for particular sounds no matter what the spelling, eg a blue triangle indicates 'sh' as in 'ship'.

Words in Colour and *Colour Story Reading* each indicate clearly a specific method to be followed in teaching the children. Although it has been explicitly stated that i.t.a. provides a medium for learning rather than a method, much of its value might be lost if phonics were ignored.

NOTES ON BOOKS FOR FURTHER READING

Any teacher embarking on a particular reading scheme should read the handbook if one is provided, and this is even more important when a specific method or means of teaching is going to be used. Critical appraisals of new methods are also important, and one advantage to be gained by reading about new ideas is that they sometimes provide new insights into the way children learn, or fresh emphasis on aspects of reading skills which may have been neglected.

The publications of the United Kingdom Reading Association are a fruitful source of such information for teachers.

There is a paper on *The Language-Experience Approach to the Teaching of Reading* in *The Second International Reading Symposium* and a number of papers on i.t.a. are to be found in all the UKRA Symposiums. *The Third International Reading Symposium* contains a paper by J Kenneth Jones, the originator of *Colour Story Reading*, and many other approaches not mentioned here are critically examined and described. Terrence Lee has contributed a paper to *Reading: Current Research and Practice Vol 1* on *Words in Colour*, and one by Vera Southgate Booth on *Colour codes compared with i.t.a.* is included in the same book, together with a paper by John E Merritt on the SRA Laboratories.

An article by David Mackay on *Breakthrough to Literacy* will be found in *Reading and the Curriculum**, although any

* ed. by J Merritt

teacher interested in this approach should also read the excellent handbook to the scheme.

Modern Innovations in the Teaching of Reading, by Donald and Louise M Moyle, is a useful reference book, providing a clear and critical introduction to the various approaches.

Most of the ideas current today have a history, and sometimes a relatively long one, in the annals of teaching. Ronald Morris, in *Success and Failure in Learning to Read* provides a brief but perceptive account of the historical background of nine different approaches. This is especially valuable because Morris has described each approach, to use his own words, 'as sympathetically as possible'. The underlying reasons for the different methods are so clearly brought out that the historical survey is made completely relevant to modern ideas and practices.

List of References

ABLEWHITE, R C *The Slow Reader* Heinemann Educational Books 1967

AYMÉ, MARCEL *Les Bottes de Sept Lieves* Trans *French Short Stories* (Penguin Parallel Texts) Penguin Books pp 25–97

ASHTON-WARNER, SYLVIA *Teacher* Simon and Schuster USA 1961 Penguin Books 1966

BELL, PETER *Basic Teaching for slow Learners* Muller Educational 1970

BERG, L (ed) *Nippers* Macmillan 1969

BOOTH, VERA SOUTHGATE Colour Codes compared with i.t.a. in *Reading and the Curriculum* ed J Merritt Ward Lock Educational pp 95–110 1971

BREARLEY, M and NEILSON, L *Queensway Reading* Evans 1964

BROWN, AMY L (ed) *Reading: Current Research and Practice* Vol I Chambers 1967 (for the United Kingdom Reading Association)

BROWN, J A C *The Social Psychology of Industry* Penguin Books 1954

BROWN, M and PRECIOUS, N *The Integrated day in the primary school* Ward Lock Educational 1968

BURT, SIR CYRIL Preface to *i.t.a. An Independent Evaluation* The Schools Council John Murray and W & R Chambers 1969

CANE, B S *A Review of Recent Research on Reading and Related Topics with a Selected Bibliography* 1966 Appendix E to *Standards and Progress in Reading*, by J M Morris National Foundation for Educational Research in England and Wales pp 465–486

CLARKE, MOLLIE *First Folk Tales* and *Second Folk Tales* Hart-Davis Educational 1963

CLEUGH, M E (ed) *Teaching the Slow Learner in the Primary School* Methuen 1961

COOK, ELIZABETH *The Ordinary and the Fabulous* Cambridge University Press 1969

CROUCH, MARCUS *The Nesbit Tradition: The Children's Novel 1945–1970* Benn 1972

DANIELS, J C (ed) *Reading: Problems and Perspectives* United Kingdom Reading Association 1970

DEAN, JOAN *Second Report on Words in Colour* in *The Second International Reading Symposium* Cassell pp 169–178 1967

DIACK, HUNTER *In Spite of the Alphabet* Chatto and Windus Educational 1965

DOWNING, J and BROWN, A L (eds) *The First International Reading Symposium* Cassell 1966

   The Second International Reading Symposium Cassell 1967
   The Third International Reading Symposium Cassell 1968

FASSETT, J H *Beacon Readers* (Revised edition 1933. Second revised edition 1957) Ginn 1922

FISHER, MARGERY *Intent Upon Reading* Brockhampton Press (revised and enlarged 1964) 1961

   Matters of fact: aspects of non-fiction for children Brockhampton Press 1972

GATTEGNO, CALEB *Words in Colour* Educational Explorers Ltd 1962

GEORGIADES, N J *i.t.a. in Remedial Reading Groups* Published for the University of London Institute of Education by Harrap 1969

GLYNN, DOROTHY M *Dominoes* Oliver & Boyd 1972

GODDARD, NORA L *Reading in the Modern Infants' School* ULP (Second impression with amendments 1971) 1958

GOODACRE, ELIZABETH J *Children Learning to Read* (in the Students Library of Education Series) Routledge & Kegan Paul 1971

HARLOW, H F *The Formation of Learning Sets* in *Psychological Review 56* pp 51–65 1949

HILDICK, WALLACE *Children and Fiction* Evans 1970

JONES, KENNETH J *Phonetic Colour Story Reading* Third International Reading Symposium Cassell pp 91–106 1968

KIPLING, RUDYARD *Baa Baa, Black Sheep*, from *Wee Willie Winkie* Macmillan 1907

LARRICK, NANCY *Children's Literature and the teaching of reading* in *Reading: Current Research and Practice* Chambers pp 105–111 1966

LEE, TERRENCE *Writing and Talking: An Appraisal of Words in Colour*. Published in *Reading: Current Research and Practice* Chambers pp 59–67

MACKAY, DAVID; THOMPSON, BRIAN and SCHAUB, PAMELA *Breakthrough to Literacy—Teacher's Manual* Published for The

Schools Council by Longman Group Ltd 1970

MCCULLAGH, SHEILA *Handbook for Pirates* (Manual for the *Griffin* and *Dragon Pirate Stories*) E J Arnold & Son 1973

Adventures in Space Hart-Davis Educational 1968

Griffin Pirate Stories E J Arnold & Son 1958–1974

Dragon Pirate Stories E J Arnold & Son 1964–1973

One, Two Three and Away! Hart-Davis Educational 1964–1974

Stories to Start With Hart-Davis Educational 1973

MELSER, JUNE *What is little? What is big?* etc *Minibooks* Collins

MERRITT, J (ed) *Reading and the Curriculum* Published for the United Kingdom Reading Association by Ward Lock Educational 1971

The SRA Laboratories: Preview of a Programmed Course in Reading Published in *Reading: Current Research and Practice* Vol 1 Chambers pp 49–58 1967

MILLER, G W *Educational Opportunity and the Home* Longman Sociology of Education Series Longman Group Ltd 1971

MORRIS, JOYCE M *Standards and Progress in Reading* National Foundation for Educational Research in England and Wales 1966

MORRIS, RONALD *Success and Failure in Learning to Read* Oldbourne 1963 (Revised Edition 1965 Penguin 1973)

What Children Learn in Learning to Read in *English in Education* Vol 5 No 3 1971

The Quality of Learning Methuen 1951

MOYLE, DONALD and LOUISE, M *Modern Innovations in the Teaching of Reading* 1971

MOYLE, DONALD *The Teaching of Reading* Ward Lock Educational 1968

MURRAY, W *Key Words Reading Scheme* Willis and Hepworth 1964

RAVENETTE, A T *Dimensions of Reading Difficulties* Pergamon 1968

RICHARDSON, MARIAN *Writing and Writing Patterns* ULP 1935

ROBERTS, GEOFFREY R *Reading in Primary Schools* The Students Library in Education Series Routledge & Kegan Paul 1969

ROBBINS, SIDNEY (ed) *Children's Literature in Education* Vol I March 1970 Ward Lock Educational

ROOT, BETTY *Reading Games* Hart-Davis Educational 1972

DE SAINT EXUPÉRY, A *Wind, Sand and Stars* Heinemann 1939

SCEATS, JOHN *i.t.a. and the Teaching of Literacy* Bodley Head 1967

SCOTT, RACHEL *A Wedding Man is Nicer than Cats, Miss* David and Charles 1971

SEUSS, DR *The Cat in the Hat* 1961 *Hop on Pop* 1964 Collins

SOUTHGATE, VERA *Beginning Reading* Unibook Series University of London Press 1972

STONES, E (ed) *Readings in Educational Psychology* Methuen 1970

STOTT, D H *Programmed Reading Kit* Holmes McDougall 1962

   Programmed Methods in the Teaching of Reading, in *The Second International Reading Symposium* Cassell pp 179–196 1967

TANSLEY, A E *Reading and Remedial Reading* Routledge & Kegan Paul 1967

TANSLEY, A E and GULLIFORD, R *The Education of Slow Learning Children* Routledge & Kegan Paul 1960

TAYLOR, E *Experiment with a Backward Class* Methuen 1946

TOLKIEN, J R *Tree and Leaf* Allen and Unwin 1964

TOWNSEND, H E R and BRITTAN, E M *Organisation in Multiracial Schools* National Foundation for Educational Research in England & Wales 1972

TOWNSEND, JOHN ROWE *A Sense of Story* Longman 1971

VERNON, M D *Reading and its Difficulties* Cambridge University Press 1971

WARBURTON, F W and SOUTHGATE, VERA *i.t.a. An Independent Evaluation* The Schools Council John Murray and W & R Chambers 1969

WIDLAKE, PAUL *Results of a Reading Drive in Remedial Education* Vol 7 No 1 pp 16–19 1972